Refocusing School Leadership

D0139866

Some school administrators and teachers have come to think of their leadership as promoting higher test scores without attending to the teachers or the students performing the work, but this focus can corrupt and frustrate the very goals these educators espouse. *Refocusing School Leadership* departs from the more traditional conceptualization of leadership, looking behind the daily routines of human resource leaders to highlight the assumptions and values and beliefs they bring to their work as well as the values and meanings embedded in the various contexts of school life.

Starratt explores how educational leadership is grounded in one's own humanity as well as in a deep appreciation of the richness, complexity, and enormous potential of people, and he attempts to restore the centrality of human development in the work of educating the young—education is not simply about educating minds, but about developing whole persons. Starratt argues for a refocusing of educational leadership on affirming and enabling those talents, dispositions, interests, life experiences, and cultural proficiencies that comprise their humanity to enrich the work of learning. *Refocusing School Leadership* embraces the more recent theory and research around distributed leadership and proposes a much more generous and system-wide distributed understanding of human resource development. Every person in the school system who has responsibility for leading, coordinating, and supervising is a human developer and leader—including principals, teachers, counselors, coaches, department chairs, leaders, and librarians.

The vision of the school should speak of the extraordinary possibilities for human achievement in our young people, as well as the talents of their teachers to nurture those possibilities. Starratt's focus on leadership as human resource development can energize the efforts of faculty, staff, and students to improve the quality of learning—the primary work of schools. This book is a valuable resource to prepare aspiring leaders, whether administrators or teachers, to deal with the way schools are currently run and to imagine and create better ways to promote quality learning for all.

Robert J. Starratt is Professor of Educational Leadership and Higher Education at Boston College. He received the Roald Campbell Lifetime Achievement Award in the field of Educational Administration, awarded by the UCEA in 2006.

Refocusing School Leadership
Foregrounding Human Development throughout the Work of the School

Robert J. Starratt

Routledge
Taylor & Francis Group

NEW YORK AND LONDON

First published 2011
by Routledge
270 Madison Avenue, New York, New York 10016

Simultaneously published in the UK
by Routledge
2 Park Square, Milton Park, Abingdon, Oxon OX14 4RN

Routledge is an imprint of the Taylor & Francis Group, an informa business

© 2011 Taylor & Francis

The right of Robert J. Starratt to be identified as author of this work has been asserted by him in accordance with sections 77 and 78 of the Copyright, Designs, and Patents Act 1988.

Typeset in Minion by EvS Communication Networx, Inc.
Printed and bound in the United States of America on acid-free paper by Walsworth Publishing Company, Marceline, MO

Library of Congress Cataloging in Publication Data
A catalog record has been requested for this book

ISBN 13: 978-0-415-88329-0 (hbk)
ISBN 13: 978-0-415-88330-6 (pbk)
ISBN 13: 978-0-203-84390-1 (ebk)

SUSTAINABLE
FORESTRY
INITIATIVE

Certified Fiber Sourcing
www.sfiprogram.org

NSF-SFI-COC-C0004285
The SFI label applies to the text stock.

Contents

Preface   vii

Chapter 1   The Schooling Context of Human Development   1

Chapter 2   Working Within the Geography of Human
             Development   13

Chapter 3   Foregrounding Human Development in Professional
             Development   35

Chapter 4   Human Resource Leadership Within Its
             Organizational Setting   53

Chapter 5   The Politics of Human Resource Development   73

Chapter 6   The Moral Dimension of Human Resource
             Development   89

Chapter 7   Leaders of Leaders of Human Resource Development   105

Chapter 8   The Organic Interpenetration of Human Development
             Throughout the Work of Schools: A Different
             Leadership Challenge   127

References   135
Index   141

Preface

The title of this book intends to provoke a surprised double take. Isn't leadership supposed to be about achieving organizational goals, making organizations more competitive, more efficient, more productive? Leadership is often portrayed as all about winning, about being number one, about achieving excellence, about taking an organization "from good to great." Leadership is also described as getting the most out of people, getting them to rise above self-serving behaviors to embrace collective corporate goals. In the corporate world, human development is usually relegated to a department in the organizational bureaucracy that takes care of things like recruiting and evaluating talent, taking care of people's security needs such as a decent salary, health care, retirement benefits, handling grievances, and so forth. It has been considered a support-staff position, not an executive line position (where leadership is expected to be found), both in the corporate management literature as well as the educational administration literature. That office, usually labeled Human Resource Administration is the provenance of the personnel director who develops and administers the policies and procedures around recruiting, hiring, training, evaluation, promotion, salary and benefits, and negotiation of conflicts within those areas.

The perspective of this book proposes that we look first of all at education and what its intrinsic properties and demands are and then look at how it is nested in an organization called a school that is supposed to support the activity of teaching and learning. That is to say, schools as constructed organizations are a means, not an end in themselves. The end is to develop intelligent human beings who know how the world works and are prepared to participate in the world as healers of its ills and stakeholders in its development.

Educational leaders are people who promote such development of human beings. Some educational leaders attend to administering the organizational supports for the other educational leaders who attend to the learning and teaching activities. This does not deny that both teacher leaders and administrative leaders come into schools as already established organizations and therefore initially have to accommodate to existing organizational structures, procedures, and arrangements. However, their primary allegiance is not to the organization of the school, but, rather, to the core work of the school which is done by the learners, and to the human development of those workers. The organization of the school is a means to an end. It does not have to look or act like organizations that have quite different ends, such as business corporations or government agencies. Educating the young is a distinctive endeavor with distinctive ends and requires an organization that reflects its support of those ends. If schools as organizations fail to serve that end, then educational leaders, both administrative and instructional, need to re-engineer the organization to serve that end.

Leadership as it is conceived in the corporate world differs from that in the political world and leadership in education differs from both of them. It is important to insist on these differences because they are often ignored in an interpretation of all leadership that equates it with corporate or political leadership. Thus, educational leadership is often represented as though it should resemble corporate leadership with emphases on efficient productivity, technical rationality, the bottom line of profit, uniform mass production, chain of command, uniform procedures, clearly specified goals accompanied by micro management of cause-effect relationships. Within this rhetoric of corporate leadership, learning is commodified as test scores; students considered as test takers who build up portfolios of achievements; teachers as the managers of the mass production of test scores. Superintendents are equated with CEOs who mandate and monitor the implementation of policies about teachers' accountability to produce satisfactory test scores—the bottom line, the measure of productivity. Principals are the unit managers who supervise and guide the teachers' classroom work to produce acceptable test scores.

The above interpretation corrupts the very notion of educating the young (Callahan, 1962). This book insists that educational leadership is first and foremost about the work of *educating*. Furthermore, it focuses on the centrality of human development as the more inclusive conceptual umbrella for the work of educating the young, arguing that education is not simply about educating minds (though it is that), but about developing whole persons, whole human beings. And if education is about developing whole persons, then it should involve the whole person of the adults who work with the young learners. That is to say, educational leadership should be about developing everyone's unique human resources in order to fully enact the educating process.

In the literature of corporate management, "human resources" is an abstract term, analogous to financial resources, to signify what the organization uses to produce its products. In the corporate context, these resources are "administered" in some uniform, rational scheme to efficiently serve the purpose of productivity. In contrast, this book employs the term "human resources" to refer to those human resources each individual brings to the work of teaching and learning—those talents, dispositions, interests, life experiences, cultural proficiencies, and prior education that comprise their personhood, their humanity. This book argues for a refocusing of educational leadership on affirming and enabling those human resources to enrich the work of learning. Moreover, this kind of leadership encourages a responsible agency whereby their colleagues continue to develop those human resources in ways that further assist the work of learning. To clarify, this refocusing of educational leadership does not mean that the *leaders* develop the resources humans bring to the work of learning. That development will be chosen and enacted by the workers themselves. Leaders establish relationships of influence (Duignan, 2010) that encourage, support, stimulate, and scaffold the necessary learning process by which those human resources develop.

With the centrality of educational leadership work focused on this understanding of human resource development, we can then explore how that core work gets integrated with the organizational and political life of schools.

Distributed or Shared Leadership

This book embraces the more recent theory and research around distributed or shared leadership (Harris, 2008; Leithwood & Mascall, 2008; Spillane, 2007). Distributed leadership implies a saturation of the institution with individuals who exercise leadership in a multitude of ways, within an institutional culture that supports and expects that many, if not all in the culture will be contributing to the work in exemplary ways. However, as Duignan (2010) argues, the term "distributed" needs to be used with precision. Is leadership something that gets distributed by, for example, the person in the hierarchical position of leadership, or is leadership something that *one finds distributed*—in the sense of spread out, diffused—through a culture that invites people to take the initiative, to be creative, to participate fully in the work of the school? Is leadership more like an energy field that contributes somewhat unpredictably to its own flourishing by the irruptions of creative energy as people work together to improve student learning? In other words, leadership emerges from people in response to the tacit, respectful invitation of their colleague to participate in a significant aspect of the work. Shared leadership, therefore, is very much about relationality, about people finding that working with others is not only satisfying, but necessary for the betterment of the work. This approach to leadership, then, assumes that human beings have untapped resources, gifts, and talents that often remain latent until an opportunity to work together calls forth those resources.

This book has a specific focus on educational leadership as foregrounding human development throughout the work of the school. It understands educational leadership as involving leaders, at whatever level in the school system they find themselves, in an intense personal work with the humans whose work they are responsible for. The research on distributed leadership (Spillane, 2007; Harris, 2008) or shared leadership (Duignan, 2010) in educational systems points to the reality that educational leadership is exercised with and through the people one works with. While their leadership calls them to daily interpersonal involvement with their "workers"—whom they might prefer to call their "colleagues"—they are also caretakers of the system of the unit which they lead. Whether a subsystem of the larger system of the school district, or the school district itself as a whole system, leaders administer that system so that the system promotes the growth, satisfaction, and fulfillment of the colleagues in that unit in the very enacting and producing the quality of the work. Thus, this book proposes a much more generous and system-wide, distributed understanding of human resource development, and furthermore argues that it a most essential agenda of those who would exercise educational leadership.

In some of the literature on leadership style a generation or so ago, we find references to a "human relations" orientation as differentiated from a "human resource development orientation" (Miles, 1965). The human relations style was often portrayed as either indirectly or intentionally manipulative. That is, the leader wanted the workers to feel appreciated and respected through such ritual gestures as remembering their names and sending them a birthday card (a task usually carried on by the executive's efficient secretary). The credo of this style was, "If people feel good about themselves, they will do a good job." This approach was stimulated and supported by studies done at the General Electric Hawthorne, Illinois, plant that suggested that workers' productivity went up when they perceived management making efforts to improve their working environment, no matter how inconsequential these perceived changes actually were (Mayo, 1933). It was as though the workers responded positively when it appeared that someone in the hierarchy of the factory was indeed taking notice of them. Known as the Hawthorne Effect, this finding was widely cited in the human relations industrial literature, and echoed in the educational administration literature.

A human resource development leadership style, by contrast, was oriented toward providing the training and material resources to workers so that they could do a better job. The credo of this style of leadership was, "If people do a good job, they will feel better about themselves"—an upside-down version of the human relations credo (Miles, 1965).

Obviously, leadership should attend to both concerns, namely, respecting and appreciating those one works with as well as promoting and supporting their growth and talents for the work at hand. Nonetheless, it is important to realize that these earlier descriptions emerged out of studies of leadership tied to organizational studies that were, in turn, part of an effort to create a science of organizational life and of managing and leading all kind organizations. The beliefs driving those studies were not necessarily tied to any moral norms. Rather, they were grounded in an assumption that through the methods of empirical science they could uncover rational laws and principles that explained how some organizations were more efficient and effective in reaching their goals (Taylor, 1911). In other words, these studies were grounded in a naïve positivism that assumed that the rationalization of organizations under the guidance of empirical science would set the path toward a maximized uniformity of leadership and productivity. Caring about people, therefore, would make scientific sense, since it promoted good work commitments, and increased productivity, not because it was the moral thing to do.

This book takes quite a different approach. It starts with an assertion of the sacred nature of human beings who deserve to be cared for and respected for their own sake in all aspects of organizational life in schools. Empirical studies may indicate that caring and respecting humans is an effective managerial skill set that improves one's management of people in order to further the productivity goals of the organization. Even though caring and respect may, and indeed do, lead to increased productivity, I am not arguing its importance on those grounds. Rather, human beings deserve caring and respect simply because they are human beings, and not simply because it is useful to do so, or because, from some paternalistic or maternalistic attitude one feels kindly towards one's "workers." From a strictly scientific view of management, caring and respect can be treated as technical skills one can be trained to simulate without *really* caring for and respecting them.

The overriding theme of this book is that leadership, especially educational leadership, is grounded in one's own humanity as well as in a deep appreciation of the richness, complexity, and enormous potential of people. That appreciation of the gifts humans are to one another is not a romanticized, Pollyannaish fantasy. It includes as well an appreciation of the mess humans can make of their own lives, the childish self-centeredness and self-seeking they are capable of, even the cruel violation of their fellow human beings. That appreciation of the dual side of human beings is crucial to the self-knowledge of the leader. Appreciation of one's talents is balanced by one's awareness of tendencies that are self-serving and sometimes childish. Those tendencies, however, are tendencies of isolated individuals. When people form working groups, the work of the group will tend to override and elevate those tendencies of the isolate to more collegial participation. Nevertheless, care and respect for human beings does not mean that the leader may not have to terminate a person's contract, or suspend a student. It does mean that the procedures for such actions reflect a care and respect for the human dignity of all involved.

This focus on leadership *as* foregrounding human development throughout the work of the school places the leader's primary work with people in a collective human work serving human purposes. Leaders can be, and often are, focused on the daily work of the unit in isolation from the humanity of people doing the work and in isolation from the human purposes being served by the work. Some school administrators and teachers have come to think of their leadership as promoting higher test scores (the work), without attending to the complex and rich humanity of the teachers or the students performing the work, without attending to the human purposes being served by the work of learning and teaching. Such a limited focus can corrupt the work itself and frustrate the very goals these shortsighted educators espouse.

In focusing on the human grounding of leadership work, the book suggests that every person in the school system who has responsibility for leading, coordinating, supervising others, no matter how few, should think of themselves as human resource developers. Thus, teachers are considered human resource developers of the students in their classes; likewise, counselors, coaches, department chairs, cluster leaders, assistant principals, deans, project directors, librarians, and so forth. The unit within the district administration with the title of Personnel, or Human Resources has distinct responsibilities for coordinating the recruiting, hiring, evaluation, and supporting the professional and support staff. Theirs is important work, to be sure, but it should be seen as only a part of the work of human resource leadership distributed internally throughout the system.

This book positions itself within the field of education. Thus, human development leadership is contextualized by the core work of teaching and learning. Learning itself is a human work serving human purposes; teaching is a human work serving human purposes. The practice of education involves adults and younger humans on a human journey, a journey that a whole human society shares as it regenerates itself. The work of learning the academic curriculum is a work of integrating ever more sophisticated understandings of how the world works with an understanding of how they, the learners, are embedded in the working of the world and how the trajectory of their individual and communal lives will involve them in participating in the world.

Students are at the heart of human resource development in schools. Learning means engaging the present human resources of learners—resources of intelligence, their native culture, youthful imagination, physical and psychic energy, initiative and integrity in the work of learning. Learning means challenging and stretching those human resources, and developing new resources that are part of their potential but are not yet, or very incompletely, activated. That is true for every individual learner in the school, each of whom arrives at school every day with unique experiences, interests and talents (both developed and incipient). The right teacher can connect the curriculum material with those interests, talents and experiences and, importantly, with the learner's need to be a somebody. When becoming a somebody through engaging the curriculum is ignored by the teacher or, worse, forbidden, then the student will concentrate on becoming a somebody in the lunchroom and the playground where she or he can make friends and achieve a sense of self-worth (Fuller, 2003). Others will become a somebody through resistance to classroom procedures, by disruptive behavior, even challenging the teacher by asking irrelevant or farcical questions. These behaviors earn points with the other students who might admire how their fellow student upsets the teacher but who lack the courage to do it themselves.

What is true for each individual learner applies likewise to the whole class. Collectively they need to engage the curriculum to find out what lessons the curriculum has to teach them about themselves, about the world they inhabit, about how they might participate in that world. The whole class can be a resource for each individual learner when the learning of the individual is brought into dialogue with the other learners, enlarging their personal appropriation of the material by seeing how others make sense out of it.

Placing the student's work of learning at the center helps to underscore that teachers are the front-line workers in developing the human resources of the learners. Teachers organize learning sequences, attend to the scope or reach of the learning activities, help students connect new learnings to prior learnings and connect learnings to student interests and backgrounds. That understanding leads to a deeper understanding of the teaching-learning relationship as activating and engaging the human resources of learners. That understanding, in turn, leads to a richer understanding of the role of administrators at the individual school level, be they principals, department chairs, grade cluster teacher leaders, academic program coaches, beginning teacher mentors, or whatever. Their core work comes to be seen as engaging, stretching and activating the human resources that teachers bring to their work with learners. That work of administrators then comes to be understood as a daily concern, not simply something that involves them in planning the occasional in-service day. That work, furthermore, has to be seen not only as the daily work with individual teachers, but as involving the creation and sustaining and developing a *system* of human resource development that responds to the complex and multidimensional needs of teachers as human resources to the main work of the school.

This book, as a text on leadership, is distinctive in another way. It is not a "how to" book filled with ten ways to do this or eight ways to avoid that, legitimate and helpful though those types of books are. Rather, it takes a foundational approach to human resource development, looking behind the daily routines of human resource leaders to highlight the assumptions and values and beliefs they bring to their work as well as the values and meanings embedded in the various contexts of school life. The book suggests, from this foundational perspective, that human resource development is the core work of the educational enterprise, and therefore should be the primary focus of educational leadership. In short, educating is all about the human development of young people, and the attendant learning of their teachers as they probe ways for their pedagogy to activate the human resources of the young learners.

Leading that work implies creating and sustaining a system of supports, policies, organizational structures, and a fully human culture to infuse the work with a rich humanity. In assuming this task, the book clearly takes a more "idealistic" approach. That approach flows from the attempt to identify human development as leadership work, distinguished from (though necessarily integrated with) the managerial work of sustaining an organization that integrates human resource development with the agenda of formal school learning. Leading in such a system of education requires leaders who embrace the value-added human dimensions of the system— the vision of what people are capable of attaining when the work of teaching and learning is suffused with a generous view of the human journey.

Overview of the Book

While I am sure that much in the book applies to human resource leadership in higher education, my focus is predominantly on its exercise within elementary and secondary education. The general outline of the leaders' foregrounding of human development throughout the work of the school is to look at its substantive six dimensions: the human, the professional, the organizational, the political, the moral, and the managerial dimension. In insisting that human resource development in education continuously ground itself in the service of the core work of teaching and learning, every chapter will reinforce service to that core work through one or another of the six dimensions. The treatment of the school's core work as involved with promoting quality learning for all its students, however, will be presented more in its ideal form, using the ideal to illuminate the ways human development concerns can be more fully integrated into the specifically academic orientations of the school curriculum, as well as using the ideal to critique some of the worst aspects of current practices of schooling. That, I think, should be the signature pedagogy of graduate programs in educational leadership: to prepare aspiring leaders, whether administrators or teachers to deal with the way schools are currently run, to be sure; but, more importantly, to be able to critique the many current dysfunctions in schools and to imagine and create better ways to promote quality learning for all.

On the assumption that human resources leadership in education has to be situated thoroughly in the context of these schools and school systems, the first chapter attempts to review for the practicing and aspiring educator how that context shapes the way one appreciates the potential of human resource leadership to respond to that context. The chapter initiates the view that the primary human resources that need to be attended to by educational leaders are the human resources of the learners. The chapter attempts an initial view of how the developmental needs of children and youth can be blended with the academic learning demanded by the school reform/renewal agenda. Teachers as human resource leaders need to have a large view of human development in order to grasp the complexity of the task of bringing the school curriculum to the student's curriculum of self-understanding—the slow, seamless construction of the self in the work of school learning. In other words, administrators and teachers need to understand the human makeup and developmental dynamism of the human resources—the learners—the school is seeking to involve in the learning process. Therefore, in this and the following chapter, there will be a generous review of the process of human development.

The second chapter takes up the adult human development of the teaching staff. The groundwork of the first chapter will be shifted in the second chapter toward a large interpretation of human growth and development from infancy to adulthood. The chapter presents a coherent and consistent foregrounding of this view of human development to the young learners' work in the school. The chapter points out the type of dysfunctions that tend to develop when this development is ignored, and draws out implications for the human resource leaders at the school level.

The third chapter takes up the second dimension of human resource leadership, the professional dimension. In this chapter, an ideal model of teaching is outlined so as to suggest a whole range of professional development possibilities for teachers. Again, the model of the ideal enables us to explore unrealized possibilities in the practice of teaching as human resource development of young people. The chapter draws out implications for human resource leaders such as departmental chairs, cluster leaders, assistant principals and principals.

The fourth chapter takes up the organizational setting of the school. The paradox of institutional life as both an enabler and a constrainer of the exercise of human freedom and creativity will be explored, as well as a model of organizational consistency that enables that paradox to be confronted though never resolved. Again, an idealized view of the human in the vision of the school is explored in order to suggest new possibilities of organizational life and to critique some of its worst expressions. The chapter closes with an exploration of the implications for the leadership as well as the managerial role of the human resource leader.

The fifth chapter takes up the politics of human development. The chapter begins by attempting to ground the political in the social, in relationships of mutuality, in a sociality that discovers others as gifts, and as responsibilities within a public order defined by civility. After exploring the exterior and interior arenas of the political dimension, and the distinction between power and authority, the chapter turns to the demanding work of the human resource leader in building a collective power among the teaching faculty which turns politics from an exercise in self-interest into an exercise of seeking the greater good for the community. This chapter on the political dimension implies a human depth of commitments that will be explored in the following chapter on the moral dimension where the exercise of political leadership finds its fullest exercise.

The sixth chapter explores the moral dimension of human resource leadership, distinguishing (but not separating) a general ethics framework for human resource leadership from a professional ethics framework for educators. By exploring a virtue ethics approach, the chapter suggests that teaching can be transformational in the development of learners' sense of who they are and how they may participate more fully as responsible members of the social, cultural and natural worlds they already inhabit. How human resource leaders practice those virtues in their work rounds out the chapter.

The seventh chapter takes up the leading of leaders starting with the superintendent of the chief of the school system. The chapter explores the role of human resource director and the managerial dimension of leading human resource development. This dimension is concerned to point out the necessary administration of supports for ongoing human resource development. The chapter takes up the practicalities in personnel forecasting, recruiting, hiring, induction systems for beginning teachers, teacher assessment procedures and guidelines (including procedures for dismissing incompetent or unprofessional teachers), professional development programs, conflict resolution, and collective bargaining procedures. In attending to all of these organizational supports, the leader brings a profound sense of the untapped potential of human beings to continue to transform the work of teaching and learning, and therefore the importance of supports and stimuli that encourage the release of that potential.

The final chapter attempts to recapitulate the six dimensions and tie them together into an organic synthesis. It is here where the leadership of systems of human resource development takes center stage.

CHAPTER 1

The Schooling Context of Human Development

Introduction

This chapter proclaims the obvious: Refocusing school leadership on human development is about dealing with human beings—dealing with them not as cogs in a wheel, not as zombies ready for programming, not as simple items in the budget, but, rather, in their humanity, as individuals with their own experiential biographies, their multiple talents, interests, biases, limitations, and enormous potential. Human beings within the context of the work of schooling can be considered as bringing their human resources to that work, resources still partially and unevenly developed, but nonetheless resources that make the work possible, and possible as distinctly human work. Unlike material resources, humans bring to the work of schooling their larger personal work which is the development of a human life that has meaning and value and purpose. That personal work of building a life needs to be integrated with their engagement in the work of the school. That is where those who lead the work of the school come in. They help to highlight the human value and meaning and purpose of the work of the school as coherent with the journey of personal human development. In other words, through the influence of the multiple leaders in the school, the work of teaching and learning comes to be seen as humanly fulfilling work for both the learners and the teachers. These leaders help to develop the multiple human resources that learners and teachers bring to the work of the school.

Anyone in the school system with responsibilities for directing and coordinating humans in the school is a human resource developer whose challenge is to lead through one's proactive involvement with the development of the potential of the human resources in one's charge. These human resource leaders, whether they be teachers, cluster leaders, curriculum coaches, principals, or directors of custodial services, are also human beings with their own personal and professional biography, their own growth trajectory and cluster of talents and limitations. It is assumed that these educators have some minimum understanding of human psychology that illuminates both their own humanity and the humanity of those they work with. As developers of human resources, they need to know their own limitations and biases and recognize when these begin to creep into their work with others. Knowing their own limitations, these human resource leaders can empathize with the struggles of others. Human development often requires struggle, confusion, trial and error, and extra effort. Self-knowledge requires a compassionate understanding of the hard work involved with learning, the painful necessity of letting go of earlier certainties, the risk of trying something new, the zig-zag path of breaking though to a clearer intelligibility of things.

The Drama of School

This chapter places the work of human development *within the field of education*, in its large human dimension, using the metaphor of drama. Everyday, in any given school, teachers, learners, administrators, and support staff produce the drama called "School." This drama involves very specific roles—that of teacher, that of learner, that of administrator or staff person. All of these persons have been more or less socialized into playing their appropriate roles in the drama. Each player, however, brings his or her own personality into the playing of those roles and improvises on the roles for greater personal expression. Some completely identify with their roles such that when their roles are challenged or changed by superiors above them, they feel that their whole identity is being threatened. Some young learners, however, take a while to accommodate to their role expectations; they don't quite know, initially, how to "play school." For some learners, life outside of school is far more interesting and meaningful. Some tend to play their school roles half-heartedly, or even with some resistance. Still others who come to school from unstructured, chaotic, or toxic home or neighborhood environments carry emotional burdens too heavy to allow for any sustained focus on the playing of school; coping with the drama of their personal lives leaves little or no room for the drama of school. Other learners will find many connections between their home lives and their school lives, with both environments providing adult conversations about issues in public life, as well as involvement with cultural events.

In every school on almost every day, one can hear the familiar question at least one student asks a teacher: "Why do we have to study this stuff anyway?" Often two things are implied in that question. First, the question implies a pent-up frustration with having to go to school at all, with having to surrender their autonomy over their own lives and their right to own themselves. Instead, they must conform to a daily regimen of doing what adults and state authorities impose on them. The second part of the question implies something like the following: "If we have to sit through this, can't you at least help us see how this history lesson, this story, this science lesson has some recognizable relationship to the world as we experience it? Can't you give us a reason why learning this stuff has some possible value and significance for our self-understanding or our meaningful interaction with our immediate world?"

A wise teacher might respond somewhat like the following: "You are busy with your family lives, with learning how to make friends and get accepted, figuring out how you fit in, how you make sense out of the circumstances of your life, what the world wants from you and what you want from the world. You find yourself living in various worlds, all of which you take for granted, not realizing how they sustain you and help to make you who and what you are. Neither do you understand how those worlds work. Understanding how those worlds work will enable you to make your way in those worlds, and over and above your mere survival in those worlds, enable you to make a contribution to those worlds and find, thereby, your fulfillment as a human being.

"Think of two examples, playing soccer and playing the piano. Well, why would you want to be a soccer player or a piano player? Both involve activities that are interesting as well as challenging, a source of fulfillment, fun, and self-expression; they involve potential careers, a way to make a contribution to a team or an orchestra. Being good at either sports or music can be very satisfying, a way of involving yourself in something quite worthwhile, something of value to you and to others. To be a good piano player and to be a good soccer player, you have to know how the score or the game is played; you have to know what the limits and the possibilities of the instrument and the game involve; you have to practice the skills and study the great examples of musical and athletic performance. In order to enter into and belong in the musical world or the athletic world, you have to participate in the requirements of membership. You not only have to perform music as it was written and to play the game according to the rules, you have to respect the integrity of the music and the integrity of the game.

"As human beings, you already belong to the biophysical world of nature that influences your health and physical growth; to the cultural world of language and arts, styles and customs, manners and morals—all of which enable you to express yourself and communicate with others; to the social world of families and friends, neighborhoods, towns and cities, a world where people both compete and cooperate, a world where people belong to various communities that both support and rely on them. To participate in the drama of those worlds, to be a player in those worlds, a real somebody rather than a spectator, you have to know how they work, what their limitations as well as their possibilities mean for living your life. Believe it or not, the stuff we study in this school is intended to help you make some sense out of these worlds you already inhabit, these worlds that give you life as human beings.

"As human beings, you are on a journey to become somebodies, to make something of yourselves as human beings, to make a contribution to the world, to fix things that are broken and invent things to address new problems. When we take up new stuff in class you should ask what lessons it has to teach you *about* and *for* the human journey you are on, about and for the collective journey we are all on. The more of 'this stuff' you allow to get inside you, and you get inside of, the bigger, deeper, richer human being you are going to become. And if I as your teacher do not help you to understand why we're studying this stuff, then you should keep asking until we both figure it out."

That answer addresses the basic justification for the academic curriculum studied in school. That curriculum and the pedagogy that engages it is intended to reveal the intelligibility of the natural, the social, and the cultural worlds to the young learner and connect the learner's journey toward self-understanding of his or her membership in those worlds. Membership in those worlds helps learners to identify themselves as cultural persons, as social persons, as biophysical persons; it situates them inside those worlds, enabling them to see those worlds as the context within which they will improvise and negotiate who they are and who they want to be as human beings.

What is sought in learning "this stuff" is increased cognitive and affective clarity about the physical, social, and cultural markers of one's identity (male or female, tribal or cosmopolitan, Christian or Muslim, citizen or foreigner, farmer or computer engineer). That cognitive and affective clarity, however, is not an end in itself, but is a means of *choosing to be this kind of individual* pursuing some of the values and ideals illuminated in the academic and social learning in school. Schools need to connect much of the academic curriculum to the curriculum of community where learners build a variety of interpersonal relationships that cross neighborhood, family, ethnic, and cultural boundaries. School learning builds those human capacities that enable them to find fulfillment in the contributions they make to the larger society. In other words, in the learning process, humans pursue not only understanding—the true—but also fulfillment—the good, their good.

Depending on many local circumstances and how the players interpret it, the drama of school can be a comedy, a tragedy, a melodrama, a mystery play, a miracle play. For educators and learners, the drama of school can become a metaphor for life. Learners learn as they produce learning, as they act it out. In the drama of school, learners learn to perform themselves. Teachers learn as they teach learners how to play their roles as learners. They learn to improvise on their role as teacher in order to reach the underperforming, unmotivated learner. They learn how to stretch their own humanity to establish communication with the young learners who come from different cultures, who bring physical or emotional handicaps to the learning tasks. They learn to connect with the lifeworld drama of each child, imaginatively and empathetically walking in their shoes in order to understand what talents and abilities as well as challenges and heartbreaks they might bring to the learning tasks.

Administrators, likewise, try to connect with the personal and professional talents and interests of those they work with, to reach the person inside the teaching or support staff role, to be able to communicate as one human to another, to establish trust built on respect for the basic dignity of all parties. The drama of protecting each person's basic self-esteem is seen as a prerequisite for all other working relationships between administrators and staff.

When these basic relationships are neglected or frustrated, then the playing of school becomes a tragic-comedy. The play turns into the negotiation of self-interest, into isolated individuals seeking to project their own personal plot onto the stage of school, or groups of people trying to gain control or power over the plot, or groups of people showing up for the play everyday who are simply going through the motions, whether to gain a paycheck, a diploma, or avoid being suspended. The drama then becomes truly a "make-believe" performance, draining the drama of all deeply human consequence. Nevertheless, in this make-believe drama everyone seems to be in on the secret. When the public becomes aware of the fabrication, they justifiably complain about the waste of tax money.

Human resource development in schools—either as a student, a teacher, an administrator or support person—is about making the play come alive, bringing everyone into the action as important players whose lives are entangled in the complex communal effort of sense-making that involves world-making. The plot is about turning learning into life, turning learning into creative action, experiencing learning as a self-birthing. That birthing is taking place in relationship to discovering the world of nature, the world of culture, the world of society as something that *brings us into being and that we in turn bring into being.*

In the play of school, learners study nature to recognize how it is their communal habitat, how their bodies depend on nature to provide the air they breathe, the food they eat, the clothes they wear, the dwellings that shelter them. Truly, nature is in them and they are in nature. They eat nature, clothe themselves with nature, warm themselves with nature. Nature provides the vitamins and proteins, the calcium and carbon and other minerals that build their bodies and enable them to lead healthy lives. Coming to full human maturity requires that they understand nature in all its complexity in order to understand how their own bodies work, and how they can heal and maintain healthy bodies. Further, they need to understand nature in order to learn how to exercise an appropriate stewardship over the resources nature provides, as well as to protect the delicate ecosphere of life itself. In this learning about their relationship with nature, they not only discover one essential source of self-identity, they discover the responsibilities of membership in the world of nature.

In the play of school, learners study the world of culture as the source of much of their own humanity. In that world they come to know themselves and the places they inhabit through the medium of language and symbols. Through the stories passed on through the culture, they come to know examples of heroism and courage, villainy and cowardice; they come to appreciate the gifts of gender and friendship, they explore symbolic expressions of human feeling in music, poetry, dance, color, and design. Within the world of culture they explore the tensions between autonomy and conformity, the richness as well as the constraints of traditions, the need for and the constraints of community. In other words, the world of culture provides all the necessary nutrients for their growth into a full humanity. They learn how to use the artifacts of culture to express their unique personality, the common bonds that unite them to various communities, as well as engaging in resistance to aspects of the culture the suppress their dignity and self-respect.

In the playing of school, learners rehearse the world of society that nurtures and constrains their social selves. In that exploration, they come to know where they came from, the ancestry that has struggled to create more opportunities for them, the tribal and ethnic ways of self-expression, of acting responsibly, of carrying out the performances of everyday life. They learn how social life is organized and governed, how the informal rules of the neighborhood apply, how human work is organized, how an economy and a polity comes to support the large-scale, common needs of communities. They also learn about people who are different than themselves in language, customs, traditions, yet who share a common humanity with them. They explore how democratic politics works—for good or for ill; they discover what rights individuals enjoy and what social responsibilities accompany those rights. Through these learnings they are coming to birth as socially competent human beings who understand the benefits and the responsibilities of membership in society.

The teacher guides that learning away from either a one-sided relationship to nature as an exploiter, a consumer, or tourist; or away from the opposite relationship, as an accident of nature, totally biologically determined, a totally dependent bundle of genetic material (and hence a non-human organism). Neither should their learning focus on a one-sided relationship with culture that requires a passive acceptance of culturally conditioned and culturally required responses; nor on the other hand, a relationship of a detached critic and exploiter of culture. Neither should their learning result in a one-sided relationship to society where one is an insignificant pawn of social history, social class, tribal rivalries; nor, on the other hand, should their learning imply a relationship of freedom from all social attachments, or a freedom to exploit social attachments for one's own selfish gain. Rather, the teacher guides the process of continuously being born as a human being through the learning of the lessons of mutuality, the lessons of responsible stewardship of nature, of culture, of society, as well as the enjoyment and celebration of the gifts of nature, culture, and society as sources of their common life together.

Educators themselves have been born into the human family and nurtured in the world of nature, culture, and society. They know what it means to construct oneself out of the sources of life provided by nature, culture, and society. Learning for them has been the process of understanding the mutuality involved in membership in these worlds, membership that gifts their humanity and at the same time carries the responsibility for maintaining and, indeed, improving those worlds. Having been nurtured by the study of and involvement with these worlds, educators are prepared to accompany succeeding generations in their process of being born to their full humanity.

Because educators are such important human resources of the educating process, those leaders collectively responsible for human resource development have enormous responsibilities to initiate and support the best human beings available to carry on the work of bringing future generations of young people to their fuller birth as autonomous human beings who can carry out their responsibilities as members of the worlds they inhabit. That work involves teachers' own growth into the full mastery of their professional practice, their commitment to and negotiation of the organizational life of the school, their bringing the power of their talents and gifts into the collective power of the educating community to bring to birth the dynamic energies and talents of the young. The work also involves the exercise of the special moral virtues of educators, namely their authenticity as unique and gifted human beings; their attentive presence to the individuality of young learners, as well as to the complex and fragile work of learning; their responsibility to create multiple opportunities for learners to encounter the intelligibility, the fascination and the challenges of the worlds of nature, culture, and society. Those virtues so special to the work of educators should suffuse the technical mastery of the skills of their profession. The human resource leader must support all of these dimensions of the work of educators.

The first and most basic dimension of the work of the human resource leader is to attend to the humanity of the work of education. Education is human work conducted by humans for humans. As human work, it ideally involves one group of older and wiser humans patiently and lovingly leading younger humans—fragile, insecure, and immature, but filled with promise and untapped potential—to become fully functioning and productive human beings. These young humans come to school with a variety of advantages and disadvantages. Some are physically healthy; some have various health problems. Some come from stable, loving homes; some come from turbulent or fractured homes. Some come with weak language skills; some come with advanced language skills. Some are emotionally healthy and outgoing; some come with emotional traumas and deep anxieties. Some youngsters belong to the dominant cultural mainstream; some are considered outsiders, different, strange. Educators have to love their pupils in all their diversity and differences, not regretting that diversity but recognizing it as a strength of the student body, a strength for deepening the learning journey toward relationships of mutuality with the worlds of nature, culture, and society. In their diversity these young people will become a stronger human community because the talents and gifts each brings make the community stronger.

This picture of an educating community of adults is, obviously, an idealized picture. As an ideal, however, it points the way and illuminates the community's vision of what it wants to become. Not every teacher is automatically prepared to work with children and youth who come from a different social class, a different race, a different culture, or with serious handicapping conditions. Not every teacher has come to full maturity, so that they bring a sense of confident authenticity to their work with the young. Not every teacher has mastered the technical skills involved in exercising a broad repertory of instructional strategies. Not every teacher has mastered one academic discipline well. And probably many, if not most, have not experienced an educational process in their own youth that linked their human development to the learning of the academic curriculum. Rather, the educational process for most teachers in their youth was a succession of teachers teaching them a syllabus of right answers in a curriculum that had little or no connection to their lives, a learning process that was about getting grades and that involved figuring out what responses the teacher wanted on tests.

This more realistic picture of teachers and schools is what the majority of leaders in schools and school systems have to work with, and, indeed, represents, perhaps, their own education experience as both a teacher and a learner. That realistic mental model of schools and classrooms represents the challenge facing anyone who would want to lead in an organized *system* of human resources development. That is why the work of leading is presented as a drama, for it challenges leaders to look beyond the present realities and the scripts that control them, to improvise on those inherited scripts, and to imagine a different kind of performing school.

The Performative School

Playing school can indeed require different performances of everyone.

1. A performative school will be involved in cultivating strong identities of all students, helping them recognize and articulate the personal drama of creating themselves—a life task that requires an openness to continuous learning and a commitment to learning what that self-creation involves. That drama involves a self-conscious effort to *become a somebody, to belong, to do some good*. These are the three building blocks for a full human life. Becoming a somebody requires developing the self-confidence and the skills of autonomous and authentic agency. Belonging—to a community, to a family, to friends, to various organizations, to socially responsible causes—involves what Dewey (1916) identified as the natural sociality that grounds a democracy. Belonging, however, becomes an even deeper human experience when one's belonging transcends self-interest in the free choice to join with others in a more humanly fulfilling sociality whereby one participates in promoting some public common good for the whole community.

2. A performative school repeatedly communicates the message that intrinsic to the drama of becoming a somebody, of belonging, of doing some good is the issue of *relationality*. This means seeing that the drama is always enacted in relationships, relationships to

other persons, to communities, to one's own culture and the varieties of other cultures that make up the fabric of society, to nature in its various personal and public ecologies, to the common work of building a sustainable social world. The dramatic encountering and enacting of relationality, however, is not all fun, not all sweetness. It involves confusion and uncertainty when encountering new experiences, the pain and risk of letting go of imperfect certainties, the daily encounters with others whose freedom and autonomy conflict with one's own. Society is not necessarily reasonable. Issues around power, bias, scapegoating, self-interest, misunderstandings, rivalries, betrayal, broken contracts and agreements—challenge and tear at the social fabric, destroy trust in relationships. Relationality is not simply about bonding and belonging; it is also about self-protection, setting up boundaries, rules to curb power and aggression, violence and oppression. We may be in relationship to everything, but that does not mean everything is benign. Hurricanes, rapists, dynamite, psychopaths, malaria, prisons, cancer are not friendly. Our association with certain aspects of the cultural, natural, and social worlds requires precautions, rules, responsibilities, and safeguards. Membership in various associations may require the curbing of our own self-interest, may require sacrifices, such as paying our fair share of taxes, recycling our trash, observing speed limits, and limiting our disproportionate consumption of the earth's resources.

3. The above distinctions point to important learnings developed in the performative school: learning what supports one's individual and communal life, and learning what endangers one's communal life. That means learning to become a somebody who recognizes one's personal talents, gifts, dreams, and a projected trajectory to one's life, while at the same time a somebody who recognizes personal limitations, insecurities, anti-social and self-seeking tendencies and the need to curb them. That means learning how to belong and thereby enjoy the rewards of affirmation, friendship, love, brother and sisterhood, citizenship, and learning what actions endanger genuine social life and the need to curb them Finally that means learning how to link one's talents and interests in an effort to promote some common good for the natural, cultural and social communities one belongs to.

4. In the performative school, learners study what *promotes life* in the natural, cultural, and social environment, and attempt to perform the positive aspects of the drama of becoming more fully human within the natural, cultural and social community. Learners also study what *threatens life* in nature, culture and society and learn how

to perform protective and restorative efforts to preserve the integrity of nature, culture and society.

5. In the performative school, learners enact *a variety of performances.* In their writing exercises they tell stories, analyze issues and problems, compose poetry, engage in reflective essays, propose arguments for or against various public initiatives. Learners engage in various forms of oral literacy such as telling stories, debating public issues in school-wide assemblies or public panels, analyzing the human conflicts expressed in works of literature, comparing and contrasting various scientific or artistic or historical viewpoints, or proposing a public policy position for the next local elections. In various skits, learners will recreate scenes from a work of literature or history. They can also perform dramatic representations of various struggles in the local or regional communities. Learners will perform science or artistic demonstrations within the school and for the civic community. They will be required to "fix" a variety of broken things, from faulty wiring systems, to deficiencies in local water purification systems, from discriminatory red lining of neighborhoods by banks and real estate agents, to provisions for homeless people in the region. The performative school will sponsor a variety of student newspapers, literary magazines, filmmaking, computer design, music, dance and art clubs, and various volunteer activities with agencies in the local community. In the performative school, teachers will work with parents and caregivers on various ways learners can perform their school learning within the home or neighborhood. Teachers will design at least one performance a semester in which learners can apply their classroom learning to a community benefit project. In short, the performative school will continuously seek to provide a variety of ways that learners can perform their learning and in the process explore with the learners what they are learning about themselves, their talents and interests, their sense of how they belong to and can do some good within the worlds of nature, culture and society.

Some may question why these idealized versions of the schooling process are valuable, given the stark realities of many schools. The argument is that human resource developers need a vision of what is at stake in the human development of youngsters in the schooling process, a vision of what is possible, as opposed to the realistic picture of how schools usually function. With such a vision, the resourcing of schools by competent and richly human teachers will not seem such an impossible priority. With that vision the ongoing development of teachers' own humanity will appear as crucial. We can see how different a performative school looks from the traditional schools that prepare youngsters for giving a limited range of right answers on high stakes tests, tests concerned with simple cognitive processing of lessons in textbooks that have no correspondence with the complexities of real life.

Summary

This chapter emphasizes that the work of the school is learning, and hence the primary focus on human resource development in schools should be on the learners. With learners and their work at the center, then, teachers are revealed as human resource developers in their work of teaching. As a consequence, teachers are seen not as developers of minds or producers of test scores, but as cultivators of the fuller humanity of young people who are themselves beginning to encounter the worlds of nature, culture, and society where they will find their place, find themselves, find their responsibilities. To grow in the work of teaching, teachers must themselves be constantly learning, learning more about each of their students, learning more about the subjects they teach and the worlds explored in their academic areas, learning more about what works with different kinds of learners. Following this logic, human resource development then comes to be seen as layered throughout the organization of schools, involving anyone who has responsibility for working with a group of people to improve the primary work of the school, which is learning.

In the next chapter, we will attempt to ground this approach to human resource development in a theory of healthy human growth that encompasses the full life-long journey of the human adventure.

CHAPTER **2**

Working Within the Geography of Human Development

Introduction

One approach to the study of leadership is to ask, leadership of what, for what? Educational leaders should be leading a community and an institution that is committed to the growth of human beings *as* human beings, as they engage in the work of the school. Granted that the policy agenda speaks of all children meeting high standards of academic achievement; granted that states and the profession are calling teachers to meet high standards of content knowledge and sophisticated pedagogy—nonetheless, that academic achievement and those professional standards will be met by human beings serving human purposes. High standards are not ends in themselves. Rather, they are policy goals intended to ensure the development of those human competencies that will enrich and further the growth of communities of free, creative, and responsible humans who participate in their raising of coming generations, in their work, in their neighborhoods and community involvements in furthering the multiple varieties of human fulfillment within a social and political context.

Human resource leadership can be and often is interpreted as primarily or exclusively an exercise of managing organizational and bureaucratic functions such as recruiting, hiring, and evaluating employees and coordinating their ongoing training and skill development. Often these functions are administered by one person or one unit within the central administration of a school district. The perspective this book embraces, however, is that every educator, whether an administrator, teacher, counselor, coach, or school nurse should be both a human resource manager and a leader of human resource development, a person who works with and through human resources in their charge to transform the work of the school or school system into a humanly fulfilling experience.

How can this system of human resource development move beyond the "feel good" impressions of these lofty goals to operationalizing the means to realize them? As a starting point, this chapter sets out to map out the terrain to guide the effort and commitment of educational leaders. To repeat, this book is attempting to compose a *system* of human resource development in which all organizational units and structures and processes of the school system will focus organically around clearly articulated human purposes in enacting the core work of the school system, namely the work of learning. Learning and all the structured and collective effort that goes into it will be seen as a continuous human activity that engages the individual and communal humanity of the learners in the pursuit of human purposes. Leading the learning, no matter at what level—in classrooms, in counseling offices, in the cafeteria and on the playground, in school clusters and departments, whole school projects, or school system initiatives—is understood as part of an organic process of human resource development that begins and ends with the young learners in the school.

This effort to map the terrain of human resource leadership must rest on some well-grounded understandings of human development seen from a whole human lifetime. In other words, if the work of human resource development includes the human resources of the young learners in the school, as well as the young adults beginning their careers in education, as well as the more veteran and senior members of the learning community, then it would help to start with a large view of how humans develop from infancy through adulthood.

Such a view enables educators to comprehend what young learners are going through in their life experiences, their challenges, their capabilities, their developmental readiness for more demanding learning adventures. Furthermore, this life-span view encompasses young adulthood, enabling human resource leaders to more readily perceive and attend to the developmental needs and challenges facing neophyte teachers, and to promote the integration of the learnings of their craft as educators into their development as adult human beings. Furthermore, as these young educators master the basics of their craft and continue to open up to larger adult concerns, their humanity seeks deeper satisfactions in their work beyond the routines they have grown comfortable with. human resource leaders' work is not completed with the successful induction of young adults into the profession. It requires working with the increasingly mature professional on finding new ways to reach underperforming or unmotivated or struggling students and to reach a deeper understanding of the curriculum content they are teaching so as to more effectively invite learners to encounter the curriculum as something that holds real meaning for them (Brophy, 2001; Freire, 1998; Nixon, Martin, McKeown, & Ransom, 1996, Perkins, 1992).

The Theory of Human Development of Erik Erikson

The landscape of human development that can provide a grounding for the work of human resource administration has been admirably mapped by the psychologist Erik Erikson. While his interpretation of human development is one of several scholarly perspectives, it a particularly dynamic heuristic tool for understanding the repetitive cycle of challenges that humans face as they grow toward a mature adult humanity.

First, a mention of Erikson's scholarly credentials. Erikson as a young man moved to Vienna where he studied under Sigmund and Anna Freud. Though initially enthusiastic with psychoanalysis, he grew increasingly disillusioned with what he perceived to be a narrow dogmatism of the Vienna Institute. He moved with his wife and two young children to the United States, settling initially in Boston. His scholarly career included teaching and research at Harvard and Yale universities, as well as the University of California at Berkeley, and at the Austin Riggs Center in Stockbridge, Massachusetts, before returning again to Harvard in 1960. Though he retired from Harvard in 1970, he continued to lecture and write into the mid-1980s. Erikson's thinking about human development holds particular importance for educators because he is basically concerned about *healthy* human development. The primary question driving his work is: How do human beings develop toward a healthy, rich adulthood? In this he differed from his early teacher. Freud's primary question was: How did this maladapted human lose control over her or his life? What trauma and suffering caused this illness? Ironically, many followers of Freud have criticized Erikson for being naively optimistic, as though psychological health were a hopeless ideal or existential aberration. Erikson's theory of human development, however, has enjoyed great appeal to many in the helping professions. Furthermore, recent scholarly commentaries on the broad expanse of Erikson's work of almost fifty years point out the complexity and insightfulness of his thinking on human development (Arnett, 2004; Conn, 1977; Coté & Levine, 2002; Freidman, 1999; Hoare, 2002; Hoover, 2004; Knowles, 1986; Stevens, 2008; Wallerstein & Goldberger, 1998; Welchman, 2000).

Erikson's work broadened Freud's theory of human development to a larger biosocial psychological perspective. Erikson understood the tensions between the ego and the superego as crucial to human development, those tensions resulting more from the cultural context than the biological. For Erikson, the ego, rather than the id, is much more the source of agency in its synthetic processes of *making meaning*, and its executive process of *expression and action* (Coté & Levine, 2002). Depending on the severity and narrowness of adult controls through childhood— which initially translate into the superego—the ego will enjoy more or fewer opportunities to act autonomously. Those opportunities provide interactive experiences in shaping one's relationship with one's cultural and social environment.

Erikson saw human development as a developmental series of learnings about how one could manage one's own growth as a human being, in the process becoming more and more in charge of oneself, enlarging the sphere of one's agency, both physically and linguistically, imaginatively and willfully. Those learnings initially happened in a somewhat age-appropriate sequence, beginning in infancy and stretching forward through young adulthood into mature adulthood, parenthood, career, middle and old age. As we will see, however, this sequence gets repeated in a transformed and dynamic way as one progresses through the life cycle.

Erikson spoke of these learnings as being occasioned by a crisis, and here he continued with the vocabulary of his Freudian training (the oedipal crisis, etc.). Humans experience challenges or crises which must be met in order to grow into more mature human beings, challenges which are met in various degrees of success over the course of a specific range of years in a person's development. The relative success in meeting these challenges provides a platform for engaging the next developmental challenge. The severity of these challenges or crises depends on the flexibility or rigidity of the familial and cultural environment as well as the physical and psychic endowments of the person, and how well the person has met the earlier challenges in her or his human development. Furthermore, as we will see shortly, these challenges recur in more mature forms in later years, with different tonalities and coloration, as persons move into new life-circumstances.

As Table 2.1 indicates, each stage or life-challenge has a healthy or an unhealthy outcome, or, in most cases, a *relatively* satisfactory or unsatisfactory outcome. These outcomes, as we will see, are not necessarily definitive in fixing a person's development irrevocably. One can repair the damage, so to speak, through more positive experiences in later stages of one's life, through experiences that enable one to revisit the challenge perhaps now more intentionally, either through therapy, or through other positive experiences in one's life. Likewise, success at one stage does not guarantee continued success in meeting future challenges. Table 2.1 indicates when these

Table 2.1 Life-Cycle Challenges and Strengths to be Developed

Erikson's Eight Stages of Human Development

Stage	EGO Development Outcomes	Resulting Strengths
Infancy	Trust vs. Mistrust	Drive & Hope
Early Childhood	Autonomy vs. Shame	Self-control, courage, will
Play Age	Initiative vs. Guilt	Purpose, Imagination
School Age	Industry vs. Inferiority	Method + Competence
Adolescence	Identity vs. Role Confusion	Consistency+ Fidelity
Young Adult	Intimacy + Solidarity vs. Isolation	Affiliation + Love
Middle Adulthood	Generativity vs. Self-absorption or stagnation	Production + Care
Late Adulthood	Integrity vs. Despair	Wisdom

crises or challenges originally occur though they may be implied in earlier challenges, and will reoccur throughout one's life's journey.

These challenges begin during infancy with the *challenge to trust* the mother's constancy of care and attention to the infant's basic needs. That trust in the mother lays the foundation for trusting other human beings in one's life, and for trusting the basic beneficence of one's world. It also establishes a foundational understanding that one's life *is inescapably relational*, that independence from relationships is not an option for a healthy and satisfying human life. Insecurity in one's relationships, however, is never decisively overcome, due both to the ego's drive for omnipotence, and due to the vicissitudes of life and fluctuating disappointments in one's relationships.

Many parents are familiar with the "terrible two's" when children begin to assert their autonomy, often in frustrating and unpredictable ways. The child's most frequent response is,

"No." That translates as "I won't do what *you* want. *I'll* do the choosing." As their physical mobility and language mastery develops, the relatively autonomous child will then begin to explore the limits and boundaries of her or his environment, physical and imaginary, cultural, and sexual. Again, the child takes the initiative in exploring the various *relationships* within the environment, relationships that continue to communicate information about her or his identity and the social expectations of the immediate family and community that provide for a satisfying mutuality of relationships.

As the child experiences primary and middle school during the latency years, the youngster tries out a variety of tools, and tool-using processes, whether those involve sophisticated technology (computer games, playstation, Internet searches), craft or artistic skills (playing the piano or learning step-dancing), athletic skills (dribbling a soccer ball or basketball, playing hop-scotch or skipping rope), or a range of hobbies (chess, boy/girl scouts, co-curriculars at school). During these years, the youngster is finding out what she or he can do well, what natural talents or interests can be mastered. These learnings will further enlarge the child's sense of self and of the various ways she or he can *participate in the life of the community*. During elementary and middle school years, young learners begin to develop an academic self-image. Through their classroom activities and out of class assignments, they discover what they are good at and what they aren't. If the school work is not particularly meaningful, engaging, and somewhat satisfying, these young learners will turn their attention to mastering out of school skills and interests like sports, computer games, chess, surfing, or other hobbies, doing just enough to pass in order to keep the teachers and their parents "off their backs."

During the teen-age years, youngsters now begin to explore a variety of life-long choices about who they want to be as adults. Career explorations help to expose them to a variety of adult roles. Strong attachments to role models emerge. Sexual identity becomes solidified as rapid physical maturity makes them acutely aware of their sexuality and their sexual attractions. As they look forward to increasingly adult roles in their later teens, school work may begin to recede in importance, especially when school work appears quite disconnected to adult concerns in the "real world." Connecting school work to explicit applications to adult concerns such as careers, civic participation, and self-expression is especially crucial during these years when the force of adult authority is increasingly evanescing.

As the adolescent moves into young adulthood, the exploration of identity matures into a more intentional choice of an identity-trajectory of her or his life. This development in young adulthood completes, in one sense, the whole struggle of a young person's first third of her or his life, namely a struggle to construct and be true to a self, a self that is consistent and reasonably predictable. While the young adolescent is capable of grasping some meaning of altruistic generosity, and indeed, of imagining a somewhat romanticized picture of her or himself enacting a heroic life, the focus would tend to remain on the self and how admirable that heroic self would look in other people's eyes. The embracing of an altruistic cause would be more the embrace of an ideology, a set of high principles that would redound to the adolescents' self-image. The struggle to be a somebody is necessarily self-centered or self-focused, even among the healthiest of young humans.

This struggle, however, eventually leads the young adult to the point in his or her life when self-transcendence is possible, both in and through a career and in and through a relationship. Having a reasonably clear grasp of him or herself, it is now possible to let go of the *exclusive* concentration on becoming a somebody. Now it is more possible to be a self whose identity is more clearly fed by increasingly deeper relationships, leading to the gradual ability to give the self away, to give *from* the self, to give *of* the self—in short, to transcend the self in *reaching out* to bond with another, or with a cause that is much greater than self-development.

As Giddens (1991) argues, however, conditions of late modernity such as widespread divorce; multiple family moves from one locale to another; interracial, interethnic, and interreligious marriages; multiple changes within careers and to other careers in adulthood; multiple globalizing influences—all contribute to a weakening of traditional markers of self-identity. Humans have to participate more actively in the intentional invention of themselves. Understandably, therefore, the deeper establishment of a self-identity that remains consistent around a more permanent set of values takes a longer period of time to put together within a horizon of rapid change.

The self-identity challenge which Erikson saw in mid-twentieth century in the United States as being worked through in adolescence, appears now to be taking longer. Arnett's recent research (2004) indicates that many young adults are postponing marriage and a permanent career until late reaching their twenties and early thirties. The twenties seem much more a time for trying out various identities, various life partners, and various career commitments. Nevertheless, the life challenges as mapped by Erikson appear to maintain the same sequence, even though the move into the intimacy of marriage and a lifetime career seems to be taking longer now, at least in technologically developed countries around the world.

Conn (1977) points out that Erikson's mapping of human development enables a clear delineation between the "moral" (following adult-imposed rules) or pre-ethical stages that precede young adulthood, and the ethical stage, involving self-transcending-choices involved in mature intimacy and generativity and integration. In the earlier stages one is focused primarily on the self. Although there are obvious relationships of mutuality to be negotiated, the focus has been primarily on "what's in it for me?" As one enters into intimacy and generativity, one is clearly involved in a form of acting out of care and beneficence for others, which is so naturally identifiable as a virtuous or ethical form of human activity.

The next crisis or challenge emerges as an adult challenge, namely, the move towards intimacy. Here we see self-transcendence unfolding. Intimacy does not mean self-annihilation or self- abandonment. Rather, it means the meeting of two autonomous, humanly mature adults in a mutual invitation to share life together. As the metaphor of intimacy implies, the self is more able to dis-robe and dis-role in the presence of the other, to remove the cultural costumes one wears, to remove the social masks and disguises one uses to protect oneself from disclosing the insecurities and anxieties that gnaw beneath the surface of one's public life. In intimate relationships, the person is progressively able to be psychologically naked. That means being able to share one's fears and worries, one's silly routines, one's flights from reality—in short, to reveal both one's human poverty and one's inner beauty and humanity. In revealing that human insecurity to the intimate other, however, one finds a loving that accepts that fragility and returns the gift of trusting intimacy with disclosures of the other's own vulnerabilities. Those revelations of the partners' naked humanity actually endear them to each other more, call out for a tender loving that protects and pours life into the soul of the other.

In earlier years, the assumption was that in order to be able to love, one had to bring a fully developed, competent, and "put-together-self" that could be worthy of another's love. Now the opposite appears to be true, namely, that love confers on one's human limitations a fuller sense of life and dignity. Before, loving assumed *being* before loving, now loving confers being, and it sets one free to be oneself, not only in the intimate relationship, but also in other spheres of one's life. That dis-robing and dis-roleing is gradual, to be sure, as the mutual trust deepens, as the authenticity of the other is allowed fuller expression, as the exploration of each other's interior journey grows into a shared journey—not a fused journey, but a journey of partners whose identities remain intact within the union of their lives.

Neither does that intimacy preclude occasional retreats to self-concern, to defensiveness, to feeling wounded by the other, to having falling-outs over minor or major disagreements. Those painful experiences with the loved one, however, lead to moments of forgiving and forgiveness, when the loving heals the bruise, and bonds the union with a deeper, mutual compassion towards each other's humanity. Gradually the loving becomes *predisposed* to forgiving, knowing that the human way of relationships is always somewhat messy.

In marriage, that sharing involves (potentially, anyway) as much as is humanly possible. Having a clear sense of identity that one chooses and intends to be loyal to enables the *mature human, the adult* to emerge. The adult is now not only able to share the full nakedness of his or her person with another in intimacy, but can also intentionally choose to generate new life. In relationships of deep friendship and loyal companionship, that sharing may not involve such totality of daily living together, including the responsibilities of child rearing. In the generation of new life, mature humans embrace the responsibilities to nurture and care for that new life. The simple physical generation of new life, moreover, has to be carried forward to the protection and growth of that new life in its own journey towards full selfhood.

Furthermore, as one moves into the generativity stage of human life, there are other demands to transcend self-interests in order to contribute to new life within the civic and occupational communities one belongs to. At its most basic level, generativity involves the frequent sacrificing of self-interest and self-gratification in proffering care and nurturance to children in one's work of parenting.

As well, one's work in a career frequently entails going beyond the bare minimum to a larger effort to contribute something of genuine value in that work. Having experienced the lessons of intimacy, however, the generative career person recognizes that work gets done with others. One's human and technical limitations need the cooperation and collaboration of various others who make up, however briefly, a team whose collective talents and energies can far surpass the abilities of individual parts of the team. Generativity can involve generating inventions, new political policies, creating works of art, writing scholarly books, teaching young children in school, healing sickness through the healing professions, building a bridge, bringing criminals to justice, conducting research on new medicines, preaching inspiring sermons, and, indeed, being a nurturing foster parent. Generativity is an exercise of human virtue that extends over the last half or last two thirds of a person's life, even during retirement, and can be exercised in a multiplicity of ways by the same person enacting various social and cultural roles.

Finally, in the sunset years of life, there is the stage or life-challenge of bringing one's life into some kind of integrated whole. That challenge involves an acceptance of the totality of one's life, its joys as well as disappointments, its triumphs as well as its less than courageous moments, its mistakes as well as its satisfactions. All of one's experiences come to be seen somehow as necessary for one to have learned the many lessons life has to teach, to have arrived at the completion of one's journey, where the truth is that the journey, rather than the destination holds the truth about oneself. This life-challenge leads to a form of wisdom, a wisdom that can be passed along in a final form of generativity. A simple map of Erikson's life cycle is represented in Figure 2.1.

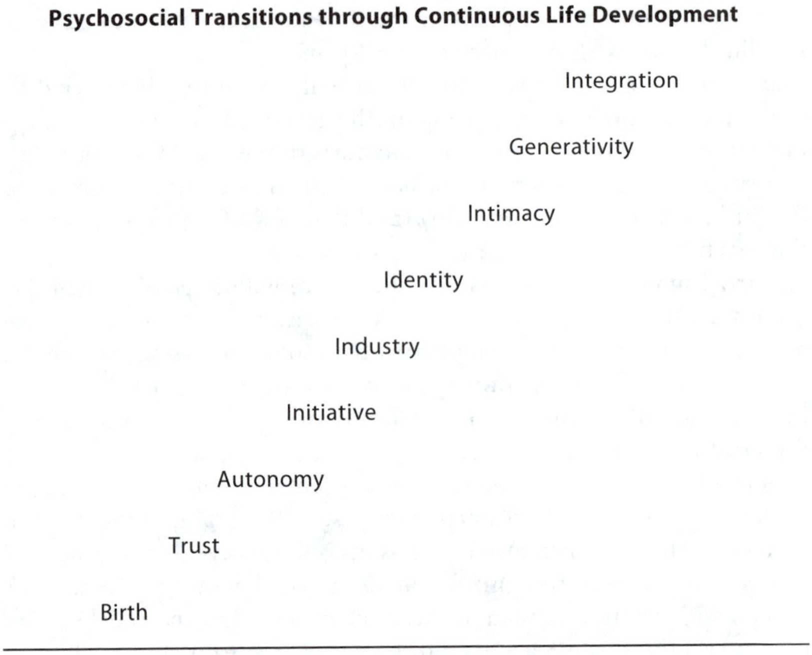

Psychosocial Transitions through Continuous Life Development

Integration

Generativity

Intimacy

Identity

Industry

Initiative

Autonomy

Trust

Birth

Figure 2.1 Stages of life-cycle psychosocial transistions through continuous life development.

Cautions Against Simplifications

Erikson's understanding of the life cycle as shown in Figure 2.1 can induce several misinterpretations. One major misinterpretation is to see the map as expressing a static, once-and-for-all sequence of challenges resulting in either-or outcomes. First, the outcomes of engaging a life-challenge do not issue in a complete victory or complete defeat. Rather, the results will tend to be more-or-less success or more-or-less failure.

Depending on the quality of the maternal interactions, a child comes to trust either more completely in the adult world, or to recognize that sometimes one's trust is disappointed, even though, by and large, in most circumstances adults and the world in general can be trusted to be predictably responsive to one's expectations. That trust makes it more likely, though not inexorably guaranteed, that young persons will be able to bring that trust to support their instinctive drive for greater autonomy. That is to say that youngsters have an intuition that their struggle to be more independent will not turn their parents (whom they have grown to trust) against them in a punitive rejection. The struggle to gain autonomy, while frustrating for parents, is not a rejection by the child of the fundamental relationship of caring dependence. Rather, if the relationship is to grow into something more human, the child has to own itself in increasingly insistent agency in order to be in a *more genuine* relationship with the parent. This example also illustrates that the virtue of trust developed in infancy must itself be transformed into a more complex and deeper trust that will sustain the relationship even in the conflict of wills. Thus, it becomes apparent that in this developmental sequence of challenges, the prior learnings will become incorporated into the learnings called upon by the newer challenge; the earlier learnings are both *required* and further *deepened* in the new challenge.

Figure 2.2 attempts visually to indicate that, at every higher stage in the life cycle, resolutions of the earlier stage or stages continue to be folded into the working-through of the next challenge. The working-through of all the earlier stages continues to need attention but now in a more mature and complex working-through of the next stage. Thus, for example, the ability to take the initiative is different as one enters the stage of intimacy than taking the initiative in the earlier stage of identity formation.

The progression through life challenges, therefore, is not a once-and-for-all sequence. As one enters into every new experiences, for example,

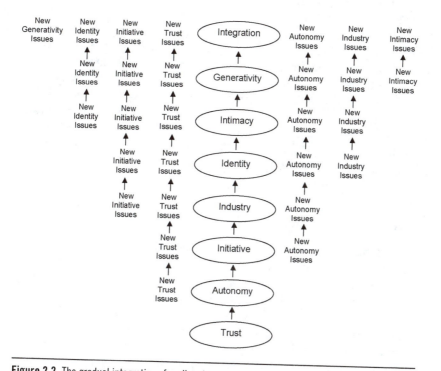

Figure 2.2 The gradual integration of earlier stage strengths into the work of more mature stages.

moves into the first job as a teacher, it may very well be necessary to apply the sequence of earlier learnings all over again.

For example, the neophyte teacher may have to learn whether the new environment and new relationships are trustworthy, or at least to find out whom she or he can trust among teaching colleagues, how much to trust the principal, and how much of a trusting relationship is possible with students. With some positive results in that search, the teacher may then be able to explore how much autonomy is possible in the work of teaching. From there she may move on to explore the boundaries of her work and of her relationships with her colleagues and students, exploring where work should end and personal life begin. With those initiatives resolved, she may then be ready to tackle the work of gaining new skills and competencies in order to broaden her professional stature.

Another example of having to repeat the passage of earlier challenges would be in the initial stages of an intimate relationship. How much trust to invest in the potential life partner? How much of one's true self will be revealed; how much autonomy will the other tolerate? At the start, what boundaries will be set, what new interpersonal landscapes will be explored? And again, how to negotiate disagreements, how to develop skills of dancing and cooking? Thus, it becomes apparent (as in Figure 2.2) that each life-cycle challenge will be taken up again and again within the various higher stages of the life cycle. On the other hand, this point illustrates the intrinsic logic to the progression of stages or critical challenges.

With these cautions about simplified readings of Erikson's map of the life cycle, we can now turn to an analysis of the psychodynamics of the learning process that takes place every day as the person both fashions and engages his or her "true" self. At this point, we are better prepared to *link* this learning of how to meet the challenges of growing into an increasingly mature person *with* the learning process involved in engaging the academic curriculum of the school.

Linking School Learnings to Life-Cycle Challenges

When school learnings in the academic curriculum introduce young people into the intelligibility of the worlds of nature, of culture, of society; into their relationships with those worlds, and into their participation as members of those worlds, the school is tacitly rehearsing ways to play out the roles called for in such participation. Those roles should not be externally superimposed on the learner; rather, they should emerge through the learning process as enactments of relationships which each world contextualizes in the activity of participating in it. The learning and individual nuancing of those roles are tentatively worked-through in the activity of participating in those worlds, both imaginatively and performatively, over extended periods of time. Enacting the relationship to those worlds involves *both* understanding those relationships *and* responding to what those relationships imply. For example, membership in the world of culture implies a growing mastery of symbols and rules for using symbols. The gradual mastery of vocabulary and number manipulation enables the young learner to participate in the various languages of the culture.

Thus, the young child sitting in the cart which the mother wheels around the supermarket and brings to the check-out station, listens to the words exchanged with the clerk, and watches the mother count out her money to pay for her purchases. The child is beginning to acquire, at least tacitly, the languages of the culture of commerce. Under other circumstances, learning the mutuality involved in sibling relationships prepares the youngster for mutuality in making friends and playing neighborhood games, that is, learning the initial skills of sociality. Moreover, the enactment of relationships is usually exploratory at first, and becomes routinized as the feedback of "fit" with expectations of the world becomes, for that individual, the gradual and flexible adoption (usually quite tacit) of a role as a member of that world. Gradually the learner tacitly recognizes that those world are *in* him or her, and he or she lives *in* those worlds.

Sociologists and social psychologists, finding broad similarities among the enactments of large numbers of individuals, classify those similarities as roles.

"Role" is a metaphor derived from the theater, where actors perform the role of servant, jealous husband, arrogant bureaucrat, favor-currying sycophant, flirtatious female. Sociologists and social psychologists use the term in a more general sense, diluted of much of the theatrics, to describe behaviors one might observe in ordinary life—the role of mother, husband, consumer, conservative, feminist, fundamentalist, professor (Goffman, 1959). Roles can apply to gender, ideology, profession, economic activity, or class. They are ways the self is socialized into behaving. However, individuals give their own personal twist or nuance to how a role is enacted in a given circumstance. Improvisation of one's identity in a variety of role enactments is an essential ingredient of the learning process, and indeed lends to learning a weighty, dramatic quality as it implicates the learner in the construction of him or herself (McCarthy, 1996; Starratt, 1990).

In Figure 2.3, we have a visual image of how the ego is the core of the individual, making sense, at an unconscious level, of the information it receives from the I at the experiential level. The I functions at the surface of the individual, at the level of consciousness, of sensory experience, of behavior and social interaction. The I is organically and dynamically connected to the ego which is below consciousness. The ego is the collector of

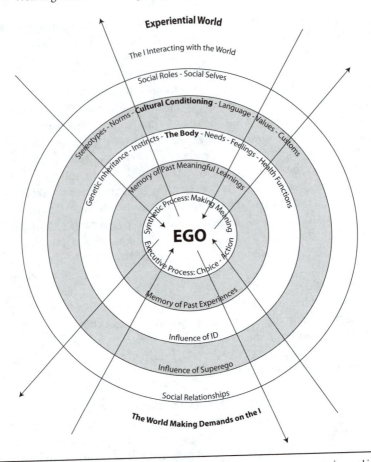

Figure 2.3 A psycho-social model of learning. The influence of the ego on meaning making, and action; the influence of present circumstances, external demands, and internal dispositions on meaning, making, and action.

the residue of a lived history, of the hurts, the joys, the satisfactions and disappointments experienced and interpreted throughout that history. Those joys, hurts and disappointments have been interpreted through the filters of the body (its needs, drives, sensations, feelings), and through the filters of the superego (what parents want, encourage, forbid; what the culture approves, disapproves, sanctions, rewards; how religion represents one's relationship to God).

The I tells the ego what is happening in the immediate, experiential world. The message to the ego, however, has to pass through the filters of acquired social roles, cultural conditioning, the present bodily needs and learned emotional sensitivities of the person, and thus reaches the ego distorted, rescripted, and weighted by the tonalities added to the message by those filters. The ego tries to make sense of that initial gestalt of what is happening—sometimes successfully, sometimes incorrectly, sometimes bewildered or confused by the surface context, sometimes finding mixed value messages as the experiential world is filtered through the superego and the id. Through that interpretation, the ego scripts and clothes the general response of a self that corresponds to the situation. That response is a response to the initial intelligibility the ego makes of the situation (synthetic processing) and also an expression (the executive processing) of what the ego wants to do in the situation, what the ego wants out of the situation, what the ego senses is appropriate and consistent with the deepest intuition of who the person (the whole person—ego, body, cultural member, the social self, the I) *is*.

In order to grasp the deep connection of understanding (the cognitive aspect of learning) with responding (the affective, willful side of learning), we have to examine Erikson's understanding of the ego as *the source* of both understanding and agency. Note that the ego is the source *both* of understanding *and* of will and action. This point is often missed in the psychological literature that tends to locate understanding in "the mind" (Frawley, 1997). "Mind," however, is as much an abstraction as is "ego." Both are heuristic categories used to interpret and explain the functioning of human beings. The category of mind, however, often connotes an impersonal, information- processing mechanism, separate from emotion and affect, the latter interpreted as found in "the body" (as in mind-body dualisms, often found in the advice, "Think with your mind, not with your body."). By placing the activity of sense-making, of meaning-construction in the ego, Erikson is suggesting the immediacy of knowledge to the person, *within* a unity of knowledge, affect, and choice, each interpenetrating each other and influencing each other, even as they are filtered and expressed by social roles, bodily dispositions, and cultural values.

The heuristic model in Figure 2.3 (and one must remember that it is a visual theoretical model that uses interpretive categories to attempt to illustrate the way a person "works") indicates that the process of meaning making, which is the essential activity of learning, is affected by being filtered through successive layers that have come to constitute the rich structure of the human person. Those filtering layers include not only the immediacy of perception, but the limitations and possibilities of various social roles the person has been socialized to play, as well as the cross-hatching filter of cultural structuring by language, value and belief orientation, religious and parental teachings lodged in the superego, and the instinctual and genetic presuppositions of the body. While knowledge implies intelligibility, in this model it implies a very complex and continuous construction, probably synthesized over varying periods of time, built out of multiple external and internal influences.

Note that the ego is the source, not only of sense-making, but of action, of responding to the sense being made, of expressing how the ego sees itself in relationship to what is being made sense of. When the pedagogy that presents "the lesson" only asks for intelligibility, but not for an *active response* to the ego's perceived relationship to that intelligibility, the interaction with the world is truncated. The intelligibility of the lesson remains sterile because the pedagogy seems to imply that the lesson asks nothing of the learner except a repetition of its surface facticity. This kind of truncated learning leads to an identification of learning with memorized repetition of words and symbols. Higher order learning requires that the learner explain what the lesson means to the learner. In such explanation, the learner necessarily, though tacitly, connects the meaning to who the learner is and how the learner relates to that meaning. Again, it is the whole person, not the "mind" that makes meaning as that person engages the world in exploring how the person is in relationship to that world as it is revealing some of its intelligibility.

That may help to explain why some learners have difficulty understanding, let alone accepting curriculum knowledge, abstracted from the learner's cultural and psychodynamic biography. The learner should be asking, "How is this academic knowledge representing something that can become a part of me, something that I can relate to, become a part of, do something with, be in dialogue with?" The curriculum should entice the learner to ask, "How am I in a Shakespearean play, and how is it in me? How is the industrial revolution playing out in my life, and how is my life related to its history? How is gravity *in* me and how am I *in* gravity? How is DNA and RNA in me, and how am I in my DNA and RNA? How is language in me and how am I to be found in my language and in the language of others? How is cellular subdivision in me and how am I in cellular subdivision? How are equations in me and how am I in equations?" These questions are the unasked questions behind that earlier question: "Why do we have to study this stuff?"

Cultivating these kind of reflective learnings ties the life of the learner to curriculum in authentic ways, so different from a curriculum to be mastered so as to act out the charade of learning. That may also explain the initial impulse of the young learner to embed how he or she interprets curriculum knowledge in a story, rather than in an abstract definition or a formula. In its story form, knowledge is more personal and is constructed out of numerous personal experiences and associations.

Because of Piaget's bias toward science and mathematics, he ranked this narrative kind of cognitive processing, which he called "concrete-operational thinking," as a less mature form of thinking than "formal operations"—the use of abstractions to think about other abstractions, following the rules of formal logic. Formal operations may be the more desirable level for scholars and professionals to employ, but is rarely found as the consistent mode of thinking even of 12th graders (Sprinthall & Theis-Sprinthall, 1983). Indeed, some research suggests that only about 30 percent of adults use some aspects of formal operations, and those adults belong to modern societies with complex technologies that require such levels of thought (Bart, 1977, referenced in Sprinthall & Theis-Sprinthall, 1983, p. 23).

This research does not argue against the desirability of attaining formal levels of thinking, nor, indeed, that the narrative way of making sense, though perhaps humanly richer than abstract, logical thinking, is always more appropriate. It leads, however, to the question of whether the attainment of formal logic is indeed developmentally possible (even though one can mimic the curriculum language of such logic in order to pass standards-based assessments), and, even if possible, whether it is humanly desirable as *the primary logic* for the vast majority of young people undergoing formal education in K–12 schools. It leads one to question the widespread insistence that schools should emphasize an intellectualized higher-order reasoning as the exclusive or primary criteria for quality learning, prior to more adult experiences of the need for such abstract levels of knowledge. In other words, one wonders whether the attempt to short-circuit the slower but more authentic process of learning results in a process of learning that is so truncated and speeded up as to eviscerate the rich and lasting quality of learning that is normal—that is, learning tied to the ego development of the learner.

Does enacting the role of "student" in K–12 schools, under the ever present pressure to produce "right answers"—the definition of school achievement—gradually lead the learner to reproduce in that role a form of make-believe learning that satisfies the role expectations of school authorities, but is completely disassociated from the agenda of the ego to define who one is or wants to become (Bonnet & Cuypers, 2003; Wiles, 1983). This disassociation, which is actually, if tacitly, encouraged by classroom routines, may explain the testimony of many students who characterize the learning process in schools as alienating, unreal, and meaningless (Pope, 2001; Shultz & Cook-Sather, 2001). In this regard, one can cite not only the critical reflections of John Dewey, but also of Ernest Becker (1971), Jerome Bruner (1987, 1990), Kieran Egan (1999, 1997, 1990), James Macdonald (1971), Reay and William, (2001), Seymour Sarason (2004), and Patrick Shannon (1995), among other scholars.

In more adult stages of development, after resolving one's identity, after

dealing with the demands of intimacy, and at the threshold of the generative stage, then the more habitual use of abstract formal logical thinking
may indeed be the desirable and necessary way of thinking for engaging
the demands of one's career. Even then, the slower, ego-satisfying type of
personalized learning involved in cultural pursuits such as learning to play
the piano, in relating to one's children, in coming to grips with painful or
joyful family challenges, may be far more appropriate than the application
of highly abstract analytical categories one uses in one's job, or when paying one's taxes, or planning to purchase a new house.

Connecting Learning to the Journey Toward Authenticity

Erikson placed great importance on ego identity, on the ego's sense of its
own consistency throughout multiple and varied experiences, and on its
ability to act appropriately—consistent with its past knowledge and understandings as well as its interests, wants and desires, and in response to
the apparent demands of the present situation. In other words, the individual experiences both an insight into situations, often based on similar
past situations, and a desire and a sense of obligation to act consistently,
responsibly, and competently. Acting competently implies that one understands the demands of the situation and can exercise the skills and utilize
the called-for affective and symbolic communication processes. Acting
responsibly implies that one both *apprehends* and *responds* to the demands
of the various relationships involved.

When this organic response of the whole person (ego and its memory,
body, cultural guidelines and formats, role enactments of specific selves,
and the agency of the I) is harmoniously and accurately responsive to the
situation being experienced, the person derives a sense of *authenticity* in
his or her activity. That is to say, the ego has a sense of competent expression of the *real* person one is. In that expression there is a sense that one's
actions are consistent not only with how one understands who one is, but
also with *who one wants to be*. It is as though the ego, in its synthetic and
executive functions has more fully surfaced, has become conscious of itself
in enacting its agency. What the person has said or done or chosen "feels
right in my gut," even though the act may draw disapproval from the other
players in the drama. The person has acted "responsibly"; that is, in the
inner tribunal of ego reflectivity, the person has been true to him/herself
and in the process has responded to the demands of the truth embedded
in the situation. The truth embedded in the situation is often expressed as
a value or ideal implied in the relationships embedded in the situation that
cannot be violated except at the risk of violating oneself.

Here, however, the question arises whether the person in the situation, due to his or her socialization into the mainstream culture, might rather mindlessly go along with the social and cultural status quo implied in the situation. That indeed is a real possibility, and one reason why Erikson is sometimes accused of an underlying conservativism (Roazen, 1997). On the other hand, one may find a certain dissonance in a situation, where values embedded in the situation are contrary to those one holds closely and dearly, or where there is a clash of cultural expectations. In such instances, one's sense of authenticity might call for resistance to or questioning what the situation seems to call for. Often, in social situations involving bigotry or scapegoating, or caustic humor at the expense of some denigrated group, the authentic person has to resist the expected response. Likewise, this resistance and questioning is often required in the classroom, when the curriculum presents a distorted or one-sided view of reality.

Thus, one can begin to understand from a psychological standpoint (illuminated by the categories of Erikson's psychosocial model of the individual) the significance of Charles Taylor's ethic of authenticity. Taylor (1991) maintains that the construction and enactment of personal authenticity is the most fundamental and profound ethical responsibility all human beings face. Erikson and Taylor help us to understand the demands of authenticity. To own oneself, to sing one's song, to improvise one's place in the drama of life, to be real instead of phony, to be a somebody instead of a cardboard character mouthing a script someone else has provided, is to be responsible to the truth of who one is, has been, and is capable of becoming, and to the truth embedded in one's relationships. Being real, being authentic is the burden only the individual can bear, is the adventure only the individual can live, is the satisfaction and fulfillment only the individual can enjoy.

Make-believe learning in the pursuit of someone else's approval, when reinforced over twelve to eighteen years of schooling, can induce a habit of mindless inauthenticity. When young people are exposed to inauthentic learning for twelve or more years then it is little wonder that at the final bell of every day, and on the last day of school every year, so many young people depart with such feelings of emancipation. Freed from the constraints of school, they are free to be themselves. For many "successful" students enmeshed in a system of inauthentic learning, however, despite their grades and test scores, their relationships to the natural, social, or cultural world remain impoverished, and thus, they hardly know who they are.

The understanding of learning as involving the integration of ego development with cognitive development, and in turn, the challenge of teachers to advocate for that integration is, by and large, absent from the discourse around pedagogy and school renewal in teacher preparation programs, and indeed from the evaluation of the effectiveness of regular classroom teaching. It is the 600-pound gorilla sitting in the classroom that is consistently ignored by the policy community, until some sensational news story raises momentarily troubling questions about the sources of violence, drugs, homophobia, nervous breakdowns, bullying, weapons, bulimia, dropouts, suicide, and the persistence of the achievement gap in schools.

Hard Questions

The burden of this chapter is to question whether teachers adequately integrate concerns for the psychosocial development of learners with their pedagogical approach to curriculum. Are teacher preparation programs even raising the question with teachers-to-be in their university classrooms about their own personal connection to the knowledge they are called upon to teach; raising the question about their own rights and responsibilities, as ethically responsible teachers, to lead students to a "something more" to be learned from the texts they are required to "master"; to allow students time—the opportunity to learn—for what, at their stage of cognitive and affective development, is possible for them to understand?

Should schools continue to promote the schizophrenic split between cognitive and psychosocial development among learners, a split to be found in the practice of relegating student "problems" in psychological development to the work of counselors and teachers of emotionally disturbed and behavior disorder children, as though psychosocial development becomes a school concern only in its pathological manifestations, as though for "normal children" teachers can continue to educate their minds, irrespective of that "other journey."

Summary

Undoubtedly Erikson's map of healthy human growth over the span of a human life will continue to be refined, corrected, expanded by other scholars of human psychology and anthropology. Women's studies have already amplified our understanding of women's distinctive life experiences, and scholarship in race and ethnic studies are similarly providing insights into the diverse patterns of human development contextualized by race and ethnic circumstances. For our purposes, however, Erikson's basic mapping of the life-cycle terrain offers a useful, however incomplete, perspective for human resource development within the context of formal education institutions.

The journey toward a full humanity, toward a fully mature and healthy adulthood can be understood as involving the meeting of initial *and repeated* challenges of trust, autonomy, initiative, industry, identity, intimacy, generativity and integration. For every person, however, there is the unique personal journey, influenced by one's biological and cultural inheritance, by the politics of family, neighborhood and tribe, by happenstance of accident, luck, warfare, poverty or privilege, talents and handicaps, dispositions and dreams, opportunities or dead-end experiments. Thus, the successful or unsuccessful meeting of those life-cycle challenges remains unique for every person at every stage of life.

The work of human resource leadership in education is therefore complex and multifaceted, involving professional, political, organizational, moral, and technical dimensions. Always, however, it remains work with humans by humans for human purposes. Because of this basic premise, an introduction to the work of leadership as human resource development begins with and continuously refers to the human journey and the need to help humans integrate elements of that journey into their work of educating and becoming educated. In succeeding chapters we will attempt to apply the lessons this overview provides to the various demands of the work of human resource development.

CHAPTER 3

Foregrounding Human Development in Professional Development

Introduction

This chapter takes up leadership in education as cultivating the continuous growth in professional competence of the teaching force. That is to say, we want to focus on the cultivation of human development inside the structure of the professional development of teachers. Because teachers belong to a profession, they are expected to bring to their work a familiarity with the theories and best pedagogical practices that bear on the professional practice of teaching. Likewise, the profession of teaching requires grounding in the academic disciplines that make up the content of curriculum they will be teaching. Further, the profession of teaching requires grounding in theories of learning and human development that enable teachers to design diverse learning activities appropriate to the cognitive and psychosocial developmental levels of their students.

Beyond that grounding, the profession of teaching requires sufficient understanding of social policy and the history of education so as to grasp the large purposes served by a system of public education, purposes such as the preparation of the nation's youth to participate as responsible members of a diverse, democratic society within the framework of an interconnected global community. Those purposes encompass the general preparation for fulfilling work and careers, as well as the continued learning and participation in fulfilling cultural involvements as adults. This implies that teachers as professionals serve not only the academic learning agenda of children and youth, but also their social, cultural, and political learning as it applies to their current development as human beings. To say the least, the expectations the public holds for the practice of the profession of teaching are complex, daunting, and neigh impossible to fulfill.

The profession of teaching, however, also assumes that the work of learning is work performed by learners. In other words, learners are not empty vessels into which teachers pour knowledge, values, and beliefs; nor are they passive robots to be programmed with the proper academic skills and understandings, political beliefs, and cultural dispositions. Learning is a cooperative venture, enabled, cultivated, guided, and assessed by professional teachers, but ultimately produced and performed by the learner (Elmore, 2004). Thus, the learner has something to say about what he or she will make out of the teacher's efforts to teach. The results of the work of teachers are not under the singular control of the teacher; the background, dispositions, and readiness to learn of the learners very much influence the progress of the teaching-learning activity, sometimes enriching, sometimes curtailing the outcomes. Thus, unlike other professions in which the professional produces the results for the client, the teaching profession requires and assumes a working relationship with the client in which their collaborative work together produces—more or less—the desired results, depending on the influence of many contextual variables. A crucial one of those variables, of course, is the professional competence of the teacher. That competence is the focus of this chapter.

Clarifying the Focus on Professional Competence

Schools of Education within universities attend to the basic competencies of the profession of teaching, those competencies enumerated above: knowledge of the content of the curriculum areas they will be teaching; knowledge of learning and human development theories and research; knowledge of a variety of effective pedagogical strategies that research has identified; knowledge of the large civic and cultural purposes served by the schools in which they will work. When beginning teachers start their careers working in schools, however, they still have much to learn about refining those general competencies in order to become effective practitioners of their profession.

Initially they have to achieve a level of competence in performing the expected tasks of teaching such that schools can offer them "professional status." In many settings that translates into a permanent license to teach, and a tenured position on the teaching faculty within a school system. The pre-tenure period for beginning teachers is roughly similar to the "residency" period for beginning doctors, a time when they are to learn how to marry much of what they have learned in their university courses to the practical complexities of each situation they encounter in their practice of their profession (Schon, 1987). Danielson and McGreal (2000) provide a usable model of core competencies, along with operational descriptors that most school systems would accept as evidence of adequate professional competence for achieving "professional status." Administrators charged with designing and monitoring a system of professional development for beginning teachers can be guided by this model. As we will see in chapter 7, the work of human resource development with beginning teachers involves specific technical functions and skills. For the moment, we will leave this important work with beginning teachers to that later chapter and concentrate on the continuing development of professional competence for those experienced teachers with professional status.

There are many useful books about the professional development of teachers (see Guskey & Huberman, 1995; Joyce & Showers, 2002). Some suggest strategies tied to stages of teachers' careers, some focus exclusively on teacher supervision and evaluation schemes (Danielson & McGreal, 2000), some tie professional development to building school wide capacities linked to closing the achievement gap (Elmore, 2000). Others propose ongoing discussions among teams of teachers about student work and criteria for grading it. Rather than attempt to create a synthesis of the best approaches, strategies, designs, and systems of professional development, I want to go in another direction. I want first to explore what the profession means by learning, for that activity lies at the heart of what the practice of teaching attempts to influence.

The Cultivation of Learning

The heart and soul of the profession of teaching is the cultivation of learning (Starratt, 2003). The word cultivation involves a metaphor taken from the work of agriculture. It suggests that the teacher is somewhat like the gardener who aerates the soil, provides supports for the shrubs and plants to hold on to, prunes them, waters them, and weeds the soil around them. It suggests as well that the teacher is a *culturing* resource and model, providing critical appraisal of the learners' work the way cultural critics would, relating their work to criteria of style and grace, logic and clarity, robustness and sophistication, simplicity and integrity.

The phrase, "cultivation of learning," emphasizes that the work of the teacher is focused on learning. But what do we mean by learning? Do we think of learning as developing skills such as decoding skills in reading, composition skills in writing, rhetorical skills in speaking, skills of observation and measurement in science, skills of memorizing vocabulary and correct spelling? Learning involves skill development, to be sure, but that is not all. Learning also involves the mastery of bodies of information, such that we can correctly sequence the battle scenes at Gettysburg and Thermopile; list the elements in the periodic table; articulate definitions of democracy, capitalism, the industrial revolution, and cancer; list the sequence of presidents of the United States, and the names and locations of the capitals of South America. Learning requires the "storage and retrieval" of information. But again, that is not all.

When we speak of teaching as cultivating learning, we also mean engaging something larger than skills and information. We mean that teaching cultivates literacy, cultivates character, cultivates taste, cultivates civic dispositions; cultivates generous understandings of the processes and patterns in nature, social life, and cultural life; cultivates ideals, cultivates a sense of community, cultivates commitments to responsibilities.

We can see from the above examples that learning is sometimes thought of as an activity, as a verb, and sometimes as the results of that activity, as a noun. As a noun, we often equate learning with the knowledge we acquire in the activity, the verb of learning. As a verb, learning happens over time, leading from the relative unfamiliarity and otherness of what we are studying to the increasing familiarity with and connection to what we are studying, until we begin to recognize that we "know" something about what we are studying, we see it as an example of something else we know under a certain category or within certain relationships. We say, "I'm learning what the Industrial Revolution was all about," and mean that we are getting to know some of the component historical parts of the Industrial Revolution and their mutual relationships that make up what we mean by the abstract term, the Industrial Revolution.

Learning is thus equated with the knowledge being acquired or absorbed. Often that knowledge results from our asking, tacitly, various questions of the object of our study: What is this? How does it work? Can I take this apart and look inside? Is this like anything I already know… what's it like? Is this part of a story? What do I know this thing isn't? What sort of clues does this thing give me about how to make sense of it? How does it feel; how does it sound; what's it connected to? What happens when I move it this way, place it against this, put it under a microscope, listen to it with a stethoscope, cut it in half with a scalpel, shake it, shout at it, sing to it? These questions, of course, point to some of the "inquiry skills" or "study skills" that are learned along the way, skills and methodologies that are tools for conducting inquiry.

Notice, however, that the way we have posed the questions above, places the learner in control of the material being studied. The learner is like a police detective with the authority to intrude into an event and require that people answer her or his questions. The detective's search warrant authorizes poking around in people's privacy, looking in closets and file cabinets, subjecting their clothing to laboratory tests, checking their telephone and computer usage. This is an unequal relationship between the inquirer and the inquired about. It is not a good metaphor for learning.

Instead, we might think about the learning situation as involving an explorer in a foreign land. The explorer has to learn his or her way in a much more dialogical fashion, taking time to listen to the inhabitants of the foreign land, acquire their language, let their customs speak to him of their values, slowly infer the patterns of their relationships with one another and with their environment. In this dialogical relationship, the intelligibility inherent in the evidence talks back to the explorer's intelligence.

All too often the constructivist approach to learning seems to imply that the learner constructs the intelligibility of the known simply and directly out of the learner's mental capacities. A more balanced understanding of constructivist learning would seem to posit the intelligence of the learner (that composite of all that she already knows as well as the methods she has acquired for questioning the "data") listening to the object of study talk back to her, so to speak, as the object (or subject) reveals more and more of its own natural or constructed intelligibility, which in turn is a sign of the intelligence inhering in the object in its own right, which the learner's methods of inquiry have already led her to expect, possibly, to find (Polanyi, 1966). Further assumptions about the knowledge in the curriculum and its relationship to the learner shape the teacher's pedagogy, as the following distinctions make clear.

Knowledge as Independent, Dependent, and Interior

Tom Sergiovanni (2001) proposes helpful distinctions between assumptions about knowledge. He suggests that some teachers think about *knowledge as standing above the learner*; some think of the *learner as standing above the knowledge*; still others think of *knowledge as something inside the learner*. When we think of the content knowledge of the curriculum the teacher is supposed to know, we can view it from each of those assumptions and see the implications for their professional development that flow from each assumption.

Content knowledge, for example, about Shakespeare or about genetic biology can be thought of as something standing above the teacher. It is knowledge "out there"; it is knowledge standing on its own, in textbooks, in libraries, on the Internet, in the research findings of scholars. The job of the teacher is to absorb it as it is, with its scientific or aesthetic framing apparatus, its definitions, its research methodology, its canonical grammar. Once the teacher has absorbed, mastered, accumulated all this content knowledge, the teacher shapes this knowledge into a digestible and manageable logic called the school curriculum (or has this done by a textbook publisher) for the learners to master, absorb, accumulate. The students' expression of that mastery is revealed in the students' ability to get the right answers on the test, which supposedly reflect that content area as it is "out there," uncontaminated by students' subjective interpretations and cultural applications. We see this somewhat reflected in the "Teaching for Understanding Curriculum," with its categories of dimensions of understanding (knowledge, method, purpose, and forms) and levels of understanding (naïve, novice, apprentice, and master) implying the gradual mastery of an academic discipline (Wiske, 1998).

For others, content knowledge still remains outside the learner, standing on its own, a true reflection of some aspect of reality. The teacher, however, as the professional educator, stands above this knowledge and decides to use it in a variety of ways, sometimes in a cross disciplinary lesson ("King Henry and the Working Class," "Shakespeare's sense of Science"), sometimes in a thematically organized unit ("Patriotism in Shakespeare, in Rupert Brooke, in Margaret Thatcher") and sometimes as a stand-alone lesson (a literary analysis of the *Merchant of Venice*). The teacher as the professional educator knows which pieces to pick and choose for certain grade levels: DNA in dinosaurs for second graders, in insects for fifth graders, in microbes for tenth graders. Learners will follow the same approach to these content areas of biology: definitions, methodology for studying genetics, identification of genetic reproductive patters, evolutionary genetic variations, and so forth, but in more simplified form for the earlier years.

A possible third assumption about content knowledge is that though the content knowledge might be stimulated from the canonized knowledge out there, it doesn't remain out there. It becomes the learner's knowledge; it enters into the learner's understanding of her or himself; it situates the learner in the natural, cultural, or social world, it is inside the learner; it becomes a part of her; she also grasps the mutuality of knowledge, she sees herself as inside the knowledge. The learner may continue to feed and enrich that inside knowledge with further study of other knowledge sources. There is a dialogue between the knower and the known. The intelligibility of the known enhances the intelligibility of the knower. In naming the known, moreover, the knower is implicated in a relationship of responsibility to the known, a responsibility to name it truly, accurately, in its clear—at least for the moment—meaning. But that meaning does not stand totally outside the knower. The meaning of the known is also *what it means to me*, not in a whimsical, arbitrary way, but in a way that implicates me in the relationship to the known and in the integrity of announcing what it means to me. Thus, the knowledge gained through the learning process is *necessarily* personal, at least *partly* subjective, while at the same time capable of being presented in its public sense.

From this third perspective—and this is the perspective on learning that ties it to the intrinsically moral character of learning—*everything* within the biophysical, the cultural, the social worlds has within it some form of intelligence, whether that is found in its genetic or cellular intelligence, the intelligence revealed in a human artifact, the intelligible patterns of human association. That intelligibility may have been discovered by someone else and enunciated in a theory, an interpretation, a formula. Nevertheless, in coming to know some aspect of reality, the knower has to come to know that reality in some kind of personal appropriation of that reality's intelligibility. Otherwise, all the knower would know is the formula, the theory in its verbal or mathematical expression, but not apprehend the reality those expressions pointed to. The knowledge would be of the name, but not of the reality behind the name. Without that dialogue with reality, mediated through language, theoretical frameworks, or formulae, then the intelligibility of that reality does not engage the intelligibility of the knower, for it does not illuminate any relationship with the knower's reality. The knower needs to understand that relationship if the knowledge is to mean something to the knower. Otherwise, what is the point of learning anything?

What we have said about the learner taking knowledge inside of him or herself in a dialogue between intelligences applies equally to the teacher who, before becoming a teacher, has to go through the same process of learning. Thus, "Shakespeare" is not only a corpus of poems and plays that sits on a library shelf, a body of work the teacher has read, memorized, analyzed, critiqued, perhaps even played a part in a production of. Shakespeare is now inside the teacher. Romeo, Lear, Falstaff, Richard, Hamlet, Ophelia, Iago, Othello, Cleopatra, Lady Macbeth have entered the teacher's soul, have set up a dialogue with her identity, have opened doors to the intimate chambers of the human heart and the human beast. Those characters speak to the heroic, as well as to the devious, defensive, and silly impulses of human beings. Through these characters the teacher recognizes aspects of him or herself. He also recognizes how many of these dramatic characters have become stereotypes for recognizing and naming those traits in others. They stand for the breadth and depth of human possibility, as well as for the tragic predicaments humans face (Bloom, 1998).

When that teacher teaches the "content knowledge" of Shakespeare, that content knowledge can now emerge in its transformative power. Teaching Shakespeare now becomes her opportunity to help Shakespeare speak to the humanity of the learners, and thereby increase their self-knowledge and their knowledge of the heroic, the foolish, and the darker side of human nature.

Similarly, for the biology teacher the content knowledge of genetics works its way inside. It helps the teacher understand her/himself more profoundly as a living organism in nature. A personal appropriation of genetic biology establishes a dialogue between the intelligibility of the double helix and the intelligibility of his biological inheritance. That dialogue also reveals how science enables nature to understand itself, and enables humans to understand the "mind of nature" (Augros & Stanciu, 1987; Bateson, 1979; Eiseley, 1962; Prigogine & Stegers, 1984; Zohar & Marshall, 1994). Such knowledge places the knower in a new relationship to the worm that contains most of the genetic material that humans possess. Such knowledge places the knower in touch with an enormous history, an immense journey (Eiseley, 1957; Berry, 1988) of terrestrial life which has creatively and patiently struggled through day after day after day, year after year after year, century after century after century, millennium after millennium after millennium until it had finally figured out how to think for itself, then think about itself, then think about its thinking, and, finally, think about what it wanted to do with itself (Seilstad, 1989). This knowledge reveals the knower to him/herself in a profoundly transformative way (Morin, 1999).

This kind of personalized knowledge of genetic biology—attained only after considerable study and reflection—now prepares the teacher to facilitate at least the beginning of a dialogue between DNA and the learner's mind, imagination and soul. This dialogue will lead to multiple additional dialogues with DNA in worms, insects, flowers, canaries, gerbils, sheep dogs, classmates, hair follicles, blood drops, even Shakespeare and his circus parade of heroes and heroines, villains, knaves, and fools. Perhaps the English and the biology teacher might hold a seminar on the Shakespearean variations of DNA.

One might imagine that these three approaches to curriculum knowledge might reflect a progression from the first-year teacher, to the post-tenure teacher, to the mature teacher. In some teachers' development that may be the pattern. Yet, others may begin their teaching with a more mature fascination with knowledge of the world and of themselves that their discipline provides. Even these kinds of beginners, however, will need to deepen their understanding of their discipline as well as broaden their pedagogical repertoire to facilitate a captivating dialogue with that world for all of their students.

The cultivation of this kind of learning lies at the heart of the teacher's professional work. It is the *special good* that the practice of teaching promotes. In learning about the worlds of culture, society, and nature, the learner is learning what membership in those worlds means and how his or her own best interests bisect with those memberships. This analysis of learning may be brought to a larger synthesis by referring to the types of learning enunciated by the committee that formulated the vision of learning needed by all citizens in a global society (Delors et al., 1996).

In their report to the United Nations Educational, Scientific, and Cultural Organization (UNESCO), Delors and colleagues (1996) foresaw that learning conceived as building a storehouse of static knowledge would not prepare the young for all the changes, challenges, and opportunities of the twenty-first century interdependent world. They proposed, rather, a larger view of continuous learning which schools should attend to: Learning to know; Learning to do; Learning to be; and Learning to live together. To this vision of learning, Hargreaves and Fink (2006) add a fifth: Learning to live sustainably.

The school's curriculum should stimulate these five kinds of learning as it exposes learners to the natural, cultural, and social worlds in which they are assuming membership. As they learn how to learn, how to do, how to be, how to live together, how to live sustainably in the three worlds of nature, culture, and society, they will be taking inside themselves the lessons those worlds teach, creating a dialogue out of which they will continue to construct themselves as bio-physical persons, as cultural persons, as social persons. Thus will the learning process be transformative as it "extends the reach of human capabilities" (Macintyre, 1981) to embrace and enact those goods found in the learning process. As teachers attempt to engage learners in this deep and broad kind of learning, we can see how their practice calls them to model the very kinds of learning that they hold out for their students. In the process of teaching, teachers have to learn and model how to learn, how to do, how to be, how to live together, and how to live sustainably.

It will be helpful here to pause and recognize the connection between the kind of knowledge and understanding that teachers develop during years of involvement with professional development activities of the kind described above and the psychosocial development we traced using Erikson's mapping in the previous chapter. As teachers grow in deeper contact with the worlds reflected in the academic curriculum, they are deepening their own personal and communal identities as human beings participating in the teaching of the next generation. Their intimate knowledge of the world of nature, culture, and society deepens, thereby facilitating their generativity in bringing that knowledge to their students. That deeper involvement in the learning of their students brings them a greater sense of the significance of their work and thereby a deeper sense of human fulfillment in their work. This is precisely what the leader as human resource developer should be aiming for in collaborating with teachers in their professional development. That intense, ongoing work is further illustrated in the model of teaching presented below.

A Model of the Practice of Teaching

The following model attempts to illuminate the practice of teaching at its best, as virtuous practice. The model presumes that learning is dialogical as the above commentary was intended to demonstrate. The model assumes that teaching is also dialogical. Teaching flows from the teacher's dialogue with the curriculum material, and also from the teacher's dialogue with the learner before, during, and after the learning episode. With knowledge of both the students and the particular curriculum unit actively present in the teacher's mind and imagination, the teacher constructs a variety of learning activities that will bring the students into lively conversation with a piece of the curriculum unit. The model is illustrated in Figure 3.1.

The first order of business in a teaching-learning situation is for the teacher to establish a working relationship with the learners. That relationship has first to build up some trust between the teacher and the learners. The learners need to know that the teacher is interested in them, cares for and respects them as human beings with huge potentials. The learners need to see the teacher as an authentic person, not as some distant, card-

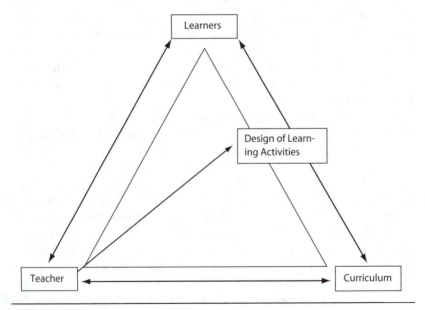

Figure 3.1 Model of relationships within the teaching-learning process.

board authority figure, but someone who can laugh and cry, someone who is consistent and reliable, someone who tells the truth.

The teacher has to try to get to know the learners as well as possible. Figure 3.2 attempts to outline the knowledge that results from that dialogue with the learners. That dialogue helps teachers know the learners' individual interests, hobbies, career interests, academic strengths and shortcomings, fears and uncertainties, family background and home context. At the start of the school year, teachers should assess each student's readiness for the work expected of them: their reading levels, their study skills, their social skills, their cultural and neighborhood background and how that can be called upon in various learning assignments. This knowledge enables the teacher to differentiate her instruction to target the interests, talents, circumstances, and deficiencies of various students in the class.

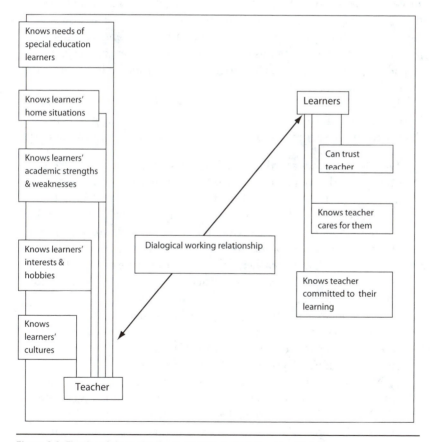

Figure 3.2 First leg of the model: Teacher's dialogical relationship with learners.

The task has grown more demanding in the last twenty-five years or so as schools have mainstreamed students with handicapping conditions ranging from physical disabilities such as blindness or deafness, to mental disabilities such as Down syndrome, to learning difficulties such as dyslexia or attention deficit disorder, to emotional disabilities and behavior disorders. With students identified with special learning needs, teachers have to be much more attentive and knowledgeable as they seek to uncover the ways students may effectively engage the curriculum.

For the primary school teachers establishing a dialogue with the learners in the class is a relatively manageable task. For secondary and middle school teachers who normally teach one discipline in many classrooms during the day, getting to know over 100 students very well is a daunting task. Some schools try to lessen the burden by having two or three teachers from the different subject areas teach the same learners for two or three successive years. That extended time frame enables those teachers to share their knowledge of that group of students and to share ideas on how to capture their interest in the curriculum and to overcome learning problems they might be having in several subject areas. That arrangement also provides opportunities for cross-disciplinary learning activities as well as for student peer-coaching.

I have retained in an unreferenced folder a story—I cannot now identify its source—that illustrates the deep influence a teacher who knows her students well can have. I present it here without any necessary commentary.

One day a teacher asked her students to list the names of the other students in the room on two sheets of paper, leaving a space between each name. Then she told them to think of the nicest thing they could say about each of their classmates and write it down. It took the remainder of the class period to finish their assignment, and as the students left the room, each one handed in the papers.

That Saturday, the teacher wrote down the name of each student on a separate sheet of paper, and listed what everyone else had said about that individual.

On Monday she gave each student his or her list. Before long, the entire class was smiling. Really?" she heard whispered. "I never knew that I meant anything to anyone!" and, "I didn't know others liked me so much." were most of the comments.

No one ever mentioned those papers in class again. She never knew if they discussed them after class or with their parents, but it didn't matter. The exercise had accomplished its purpose. The students were happy with themselves and one another. That group of students moved on.

Several years later, one of the students was killed in Viet Nam and his teacher attended the funeral of that special student. The church was packed with his friends. One by one those who loved him took a last walk by the coffin. The teacher was the last one to bless the coffin. As she stood there, one of the soldiers who acted as pallbearer came up to her. "Were you Mark's math teacher?" he asked. She nodded: "yes." Then he said: "Mark talked about you a lot."

After the funeral, most of Mark's former classmates went together to a luncheon. Mark's mother and father were there, obviously waiting to speak with his teacher. "We want to show you something," his father said, taking a wallet out of his pocket. "They found this on Mark when he was killed. We thought you might recognize it."

Opening the billfold, he carefully removed two worn pieces of notebook paper that had obviously been taped, folded and refolded many times. The teacher knew without looking that the papers were the ones on which she had listed all the good things each of Mark's classmates had said about him. Thank you so much for doing that," Mark's mother said. "As you can see, Mark treasured it."

All of Mark's former classmates started to gather around. Charlie smiled rather sheepishly and said, "I still have my list. It's in the top drawer of my desk at home." Chuck's wife said, "Chuck asked me to put his in our wedding album." "I have mine too," Marilyn said. "It's in my diary." Then Vicki, another classmate, reached into her pocketbook, took out her wallet and showed her worn and frazzled list to the group "I carry this with me at all times," Vicki said and without batting an eyelash, she continued: "I think we all saved our lists."

The second leg of the triangle concerns the teacher's knowledge of the curriculum (cf. Figure 3.3). As indicated earlier, that knowledge can be relatively superficial and naïve, as simply external knowledge of an academic area to be mastered and reproduced for assessment exercises, or it can be personalized knowledge that continues to reveal the knower's relationship to and participation in the natural, cultural, or social world. Primary teachers have a life-long agenda here, for they may know one or two academic areas reasonably well, but have a very limited mastery of several others. They have continually to listen to the curriculum content talk back to them, to show a side of its intelligibility that will be useful for students to discover, that will in turn talk back to the students and help them see more deeply how they are connected to the natural, cultural, and social worlds.

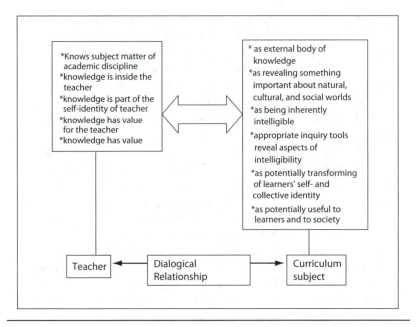

Figure 3.3 Second leg of the model: Teacher's dialogical relationship with curriculum subject matter.

One of the challenges for primary teachers is to translate their adult understanding of the subject matter into the design of learning activities that can appeal to the minds and imaginations and feelings of their young learners, while at the same time being true to the integrity of their own understandings. This translation of the teachers' understandings of their subject matter into appealing and clarifying learning activities is, of course, a challenge for teachers at all levels. Again, because of the diversity within classrooms, much of this translation will have to be more and more customized to fit various groups of learners. Here is where the five kinds of learning mentioned above (learning to know, to do, to be, to live together, to live sustainably) may provide an enlarged imaginative landscape for the teacher to construct a variety of learning activities.

The teacher's dialogue with the curriculum will always take place with the students standing in the picture, with the teacher asking of the subject matter, "What do you have to say to these learners that might be of particular importance to their lives? How do you connect to them? How might they connect to you? How do you help them understand something about themselves that adds value to who they are? How do you deepen their encounter with the natural, cultural or social worlds?"

These questions lead naturally to the third leg of the triangle, the dialogue between the students and the subject matter (cf. Figure 3.4). The teacher's work on this leg of the triangle involves her bringing together her knowledge of the students with her knowledge of the curriculum and designing learning activities that bring the students into active dialogue with the subject matter. Those activities can involve games, puzzles, memory tricks, projects, problems, reading and writing exercises, dramatic performances, story-telling, dance, experiments with color, shape, sounds, movements, measurement exercises, songs, debates, jig-saw exercises—whatever will bring the learners into some kind of experience with the subject matter. As the learners become more familiar and more comfortable with the subject matter, the teacher will inevitably involve the learners in reflective questions about how they are making sense of the material, and how the material is talking back to them.

The important part of any pedagogical scheme is to bring the knowledge from outside to inside the learner. The teacher should insist on the

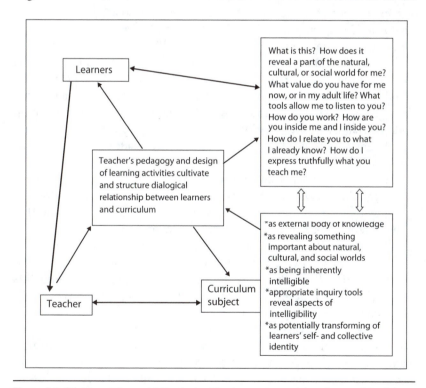

Figure 3.4 Third leg of the model: Teacher's efficacious pedagogy brings learners into dialogue with the curriculum.

learner being responsible to the knowledge they are personally appropriating and constructing. That means naming what they know carefully and truthfully, not attempting to inflate their knowledge beyond what it is, not making believe that they know something when they don't. The learners should constantly be encouraged to name what they know as far as they know it, even if that knowledge is expressed tentatively, in a hunch or a guess. Such responses as "It seems to me that this story is about making friends, about the risk of making a friend, because when you tell stuff to your friend that you wouldn't tell to anyone else because they might think you're weird, you hope your friend will still accept you." The response indicates a learner attempting to articulate some truth the story reveals about the nature of friendship, especially as the learner may have experienced it in her or his own life. The teacher might follow up with the question: "And when a friend accepts what you tell about your self as ok, how does that make you feel?" The question invites the student to generate additional learnings about friendship, not from a book, but from a dialogue with his own experience of friendship. The teacher might also ask the more challenging follow-up question: "But what if your friend says that she disagrees with you; that she thinks that what you're telling her is kind of weird?" That opens up more avenues for exploring how friendship doesn't always mean the other person agrees with you, and that one can be helped by a friend who offers a different perspective on things. Here, the teacher can also refer back to the story and ask whether the story provides confirming evidence that friendship is risky but worth the risk. The questions require the student to take elements of the story further inside to probe what his answer will be.

No matter what the academic subject matter, the teacher can always encourage this movement from outside knowledge to inside knowledge, bringing the learner into dialogue with that knowledge and how that knowledge might be in relationship to the learner, what that knowledge helps the learner to understand about her or himself or about the world in which they exercise their membership. This kind of learning process always *intentionally* raises the questions, "What's the point of learning this stuff? What does it have to do with us? Why is it important? What is its value for us?" Requiring the learners to answer those questions as truthfully as they can occasions that ongoing dialogue with knowledge that makes it personally significant. The teacher, however, will not necessarily require these dialogues between the learner and the subject matter every day, because sometimes the focus of the lesson will be relatively narrow or it may not lend itself to that kind of reflective learning. Often, such deep, internalizing of the learning is more appropriate toward the end of a larger unit of the curriculum.

Implications of the Model for Teachers' Growth

Teachers will always be refining their pedagogical skills and strategies. One of the obvious reasons behind professional development programs is precisely to support improvement of their pedagogical skills and strategies. Often these programs, however, provide a kind of cookbook menu of exercises, a new bag of tricks to hook students into learning the material, without being grounded in any kind of deeper purpose than it helps learners prepare for exams. What this third leg of the triangle provides is that deeper rationale to the learning process that should guide and shape all of the pedagogical skills and strategies the teacher employs.

Let us listen to a teacher's reflection on her individually devised professional development project to target her pedagogy towards the perceived needs of students.

> The most beneficial aspect of the process was probably the initial planning of it...thinking about it even before the implementing... thinking in my own mind what I could do with my particular group of students and my unique situation...what would be one thing that I could really work on and concentrate on this year that would impact them. And I think even if I'd only done a small segment of what I'd planned, I think it would have been worthwhile because it made me look at what the needs might be within my students that I could have a personal impact on within the school year. It made me take a look at myself and at my teaching and what I could work on. (Adams 2004, p. 113)

In passing it might be helpful to observe how this teacher was not using an officially proscribed technique based on research studies (knowledge above the teacher), but was calling on the knowledge gained from experience, the knowledge inside her, to construct new approaches to her teaching. The tone of her reflections reveals a deep commitment to her students, and to a dialogical working relationship with them, thus indicating professional growth on both the first and the third leg of the model outlined above. In honoring these interests, the teacher practices the good of the teaching profession. While the results are seldom perfect, a community of teachers' continuous practice of attending to these interests cumulatively over twelve or thirteen years produces the "good" of a reasonably well-educated person who is ready to take charge of her or his life, participate responsibly in public life, take on full membership in the worlds of nature, society, and culture.

The model suggests that teachers need continuously to improve their dialogical knowledge on all three legs of the triangle. For some teachers that might mean a year or two additional learning about special-needs children and how better to respond to them. For other teachers that might mean a year or two devoted to a greater personal understanding of the science embedded in the curriculum he or she teaches. For still others, it may mean a year working in a new team to develop appropriate rubrics for assessing student work. For teachers feeling the intense pressure to map their teaching to the state curriculum standards, that may mean developing a personal understanding of the knowledge required by the standards in order to reconstruct his or her teaching in such a way that students can encounter that material in a dialogical learning process and engage in the five kinds of learning within that dialogue. More than likely, these particular targets for growth are shared by other teachers; whenever possible, teams of teachers should work together in these areas. The hands-on learning from the group will enhance and speed up the teachers' learning.

Summary

This chapter has attempted to position the ongoing work of teachers' professional development close to the core work of the school, namely the learning of the students (Elmore, n.d.). In so doing, the professional development of teachers may be linked to the national agenda of school renewal and the closing of the achievement gap. The model of teaching presented here attempts to go deeper into the relationships teachers establish with learners, and the relationships teachers have with their curricula. This enables us to see how the teaching-learning process, while responding to clearer articulations of curriculum standards and rubrics for assessment, goes beyond the mastery of right answers for the high stakes tests. The level of learning proposed is more authentically related to the human life-journeys of the learners. Indeed, such learning ties into the large theme of leadership as human resource development we have been proposing as the core work, not only for students and teachers, but the core work of all who would exercise leadership within the school system.

CHAPTER 4

Human Resource Leadership Within Its Organizational Setting

Introduction

In this chapter, we consider the setting for human resource development, namely, the organization in which human resources are nested. Obviously, the development of human resources would differ within the organizational arrangements of a hospital, a prison, a military base, a bank. Those different settings would reflect different horizontal and vertical operational procedures, policies, communication networks, systems of authority, diversification of roles, accountability systems, support functions, and so forth. Human resource development in schools and school systems, while conforming to very general principles of human resource development, serves the purposes and institutional identities of schools. In this chapter, we shall consider some large conceptual and metaphorical frameworks for understanding how schools as organizations function and explore the implications for those with human resource development responsibilities.

Human Resources as the Life Blood of Organizations

When considering the biology of a human body, we can see how important is the circulation of blood to its life and functioning. The blood carries nutrients and chemicals to various parts of the body. When the brain is deprived of blood it gradually ceases to function; similarly for the lungs and digestive system. All the body's tissue and bone structure requires blood to give them life and strength. So, too, it is difficult to conceive of an organization without people inside the organization who carry the energy, the oxygen and nutrients that enable it to function. Schools as organizations cease to be schools without students and teachers, and—given the complexity of present day school systems—without the support staff of secretaries, counselors, computer technicians, maintenance and cafeteria personnel, central office support staff, and others. The presence of these "human resources" enables schools to function as organizations. The organization charts, the curriculum and daily schedule, the budgeting and accounting systems, the communication technologies—these are all important factors in the organizational life of schools. Without the humans who construct and enact these organizational features, however, schools as functioning organizations cease to exist. That is why we began our journey into human resource management and development with a grounding in the human in all its complex potential. That is the perspective we can never ignore in leading the development of human resources.

The success or failure, the greatness or insignificance of a school's achievement is due to the people who make the organization what it is. One can work in a brand new school with all the latest architectural innovations, with advanced computer databases and computer software technologies, with diagnostic and enrichment capabilities, and with abundant financial resources. Without the talent of committed professionals who appreciate the complexity of human relationships, however, that school might limp along, well behind the performance of a school with half the material resources but which enjoyed an organizational life enriched by human talent, enthusiasm, and commitment.

The Tension Between Personal Fulfillment and Organizational Demands

Max Weber, one of the giants of modern social theory, articulated the paradox that the modern organization is the greatest threat to human freedom and creativity and, at the same time, the major context for the exercise of human freedom and creativity (Eisenstadt, 1968). The first part of that paradox points to the tendency of organizations to rationalize all aspects of the behavior of humans within them, to create roles and rules and operational procedures that enhance uniformity and predictability in the service of operational efficiency—and thereby narrow and constrain the discretion of those in the organization to imagine a better way of doing things. Under such constraints the organizational routines tend to become ironclad definitions of what is possible. The second part of the paradox is that membership in organizations has come to dominate the context of human living such that so very many of the details and necessities of human life are delivered or covered by an interlocking network of organizations that extends to church, mosque, synagogue, to family services, to wedding and funeral arrangements, to school, to work or career, to political participation, to museums, theaters, public libraries, opera houses, sports organizations, military and police organizations, shopping malls and distribution centers, legal organizations, medical institutions, transportation systems, communications systems, voluntary associations such as Boy Scouts and Girl Scouts, Little League, book clubs, quilting circles, The Red Cross, etc. Participation in those organizations provides an opportunity to work together with other participants and, with the resources of organizations, to bring about some desirable human outcome.

Within organizations, then, humans have a chance to do something of some significance which individually, without the resources of the organization, they could not dream of accomplishing. Moreover, organizational life cannot be totally controlled; there will always be opportunities—more or less—for some innovation. Depending on one's position in the organization, one may influence a significant organizational policy or procedure that greatly improves the internal functioning of the organization, or repositions the organization within the wider society to advance its goals more effectively. Thus, the exercise of freedom and creativity within one's organizational membership can have vastly greater influence than could ever have been achieved as an individual acting with only their own resources.

Think of a young person attempting to educate herself. She can go to the public library. Membership in the public library provides her with vastly greater resources than her family library. But who is to guide her towards the appropriate readings or computer resources? Left to her own resources, she might spend years haphazardly reading through histories, biographies, geographical treatises, perhaps even through all of Shakespeare's plays. But who is to accompany her on this meandering journey, asking her to articulate in her own words how she understands what she is reading, probing with her what lessons these readings hold for her own life, for her life's work? Who is to suggest a differing point of view to the one contained in the resources she is working with? Who is to help her assess what she is learning and what she might do with that learning? Obviously, the example points to the much greater resources that would be at her disposal at even a mediocre school.

On the other hand, when she attends a school, her ability to go where her interests at the moment lead her is strictly limited by the daily and weekly schedule of school subjects to be covered. Her ability to imaginatively reconstruct what she is reading into her personal meaning structures is constrained by the need to construct the right answers to the teacher's questions. The meanings within the subjects being studied are now determined by the teacher and the test makers. She is taught to disregard her ability to make meaning by relating what she is studying to her lived experience. She learns to regurgitate the abstract and decontextualized formulae and logic of the textbook and to decontaminate her responses from any personal associations. Her creative reconstruction of meaning through metaphor and imagery is constrained by the school's need for precise definitions that can correspond to test-question responses.

Imagine a teacher whose work involves the individual tutoring of a few students at her home. Such an arrangement lends itself to a powerfully influential relationship with those few students, especially if it is carried over through three or four years (as is suggested by Rousseau's description of the tutor/student relationship in *Emile*). Such an arrangement enables the teacher to be much more responsive to the interests and talents of her charges, expanding on any given day the time for art, and on another, the time for scientific experiment. Because of the more continuous contact with the learners over three or four years, the teacher can delay the focus on certain aspects of the syllabus until the youngster is ready for mastering the demands of that material. On the other hand, the teacher may not be the kind of polymath such a pedagogy requires in which the mastery of many academic disciplines enables the teacher to point out many salient relationships across academic disciplines. She might be familiar with early childhood learning dispositions, but ignorant of the complexities of preadolescent or adolescent learning dispositions. Her students would be denied the benefit of learning with other learners whose backgrounds and learning styles might be different and therefore enriching of the common learning experiences to be had within a group of diverse learners.

On the other hand, when a teacher hires on at a typical public school, her freedom and discretion are severely circumscribed. She is expected to cover the syllabus in its entirety by the end of the semester or year for all the twenty-five or so students in her classroom. She is expected to keep a grade book in which the grades of all her students are recorded on a daily and weekly basis. Although she recognizes significant disparities in the readiness of some of her students for various elements in the curriculum, there is simply the one-size-fits-all time for learning, one textbook and one set of assessment protocols used with every student. Through some schoolwide encouragement of differentiated instruction, she finds that she can be creative in coming up with different scaffolding procedures for groups of students whose learning styles and readiness require different launching strategies. However, even within those groups of students, there are some whose backgrounds present further obstacles to engaging the curriculum. There is not enough time in the day or the week to work with every individual learner the way she used to during her tutoring career.

Thus, we can see the powerful tensions of Weber's paradox. Membership in communities of learners and teachers within the organization we call schools provides learners and teachers with resources they would otherwise lack, such as libraries, science labs, guidance counselors, and a variety of teachers with a variety of areas of expertise. Schools, moreover, provide some opportunities for learners to develop as free and creative individuals who discover and construct themselves in the process of doing the work of the school, namely, learning. Nevertheless, both learners and teachers have to deal with the first part of the paradox, namely the constraints on their freedom and creativity imposed by their membership in the organization of the school. Teachers are not free to sleep late on any given Tuesday or Wednesday; students are not free to skip second period class; teachers' creativity to teach history by starting with the present and working backwards is limited by the syllabus teachers are expected to follow which normally starts the other way around; students are cautioned against creative algebra and, instead, encouraged to follow the model solutions proposed in the textbook. High-stakes state tests impose an intense concentration on certain areas of the academic disciplines to the neglect of others. Currently, the one-size-fits-all daily and weekly schedules impose limitations on the freedom and creativity of both teachers and learners.

Those involved with managing and developing human resources in schools have to deal with this paradox of organizational life. They have to continually encourage teachers to exercise their creativity in the preparation of learning activities for learners, to encourage the use of imagination as well as abstract concepts in the learning process, and to seek continually for multiple approaches to their instructional protocols that are responsive to the diverse learning dispositions of their learners. Teachers as human resource developers must make sure that the learning agenda is tied to the lives and experiences of the learners so that their learning can be grounded in personal meaning-making. On the other hand, they must monitor the expected progress of groups of learners to make sure that they are reasonably prepared for in-school and state assessments. In other words, all human resource developers throughout the school system must address the paradox of organizational membership for both teachers and learners, intentionally confronting the paradox, not as a fatalistic circumstance over which they have no control, but as a challenge to their collective freedom and creativity to achieve both the school's and their own personal goals.

Obviously, there will never be a resolution to this paradox. But that is the point: confronting the paradox and intentionally facing its challenge is an intrinsic lesson the school has to teach about the nature of learning and living in the contemporary world. To be sure, schools provide periods for play, for socializing over lunch, for participation in co-curricular activities.

These times specifically address the need humans have for relief from intensive concentration on the academic learning agenda of the school, and for personal expression and social engagement. On the other hand, this does not mean that, once they enter or re-enter the classroom door, both teachers and learners leave their freedom and creativity behind them. Their job is to find within the formal agenda of learning school subjects some opportunities for personal fulfillment, creativity, and individuality. To accept a simplistic dichotomy between in-class work, and out-of-class enjoyments is to sustain an approach to formal learning that eviscerates the human significance of the academic learning process and identifies it with the learning of someone else's answers to someone else's questions. When this division between formal academic learning and the more haphazard social learning outside of classrooms dominates the assumptions about the academic learning agenda, school learning can become an intrinsically alienating activity (Pope, 2001). The evident disinterest in classroom work exhibited by middle and high school students facing the daily routinized pedagogy of "delivering the curriculum" can be traced back to this division between the engagement in "real life" and the decontextualized learning of abstract academic material (Perkins, 1992).

The Tension Between Structure and Agency in Organizations

Anthony Giddens (1986) provides an insightful analysis of organizational life as the "structuration of agency" (try to introduce that terminology at your next cocktail party). His analysis suggests that humans replay or recreate the organization through their daily routinized actions. Those actions are controlled and shaped by the structures of the organization, by the physical paces various people in the organization occupy, by their varied roles, by the schedule of the day and week. Authority structures, hierarchical roles and status, work routines, communication patterns, organizational identities are reenacted every day by the actors or agents of the organization. The organizational structures are both the medium and the product of the agency of its members. Organizational structures are the *medium* in the sense that they routinize the daily procedures that define what is possible and desirable for the agents to do or to enact. Organizational structures are the *product* in the sense that through their agency the members produce or reproduce the organizational structures and procedures that define the organization.

Think of a hospital. Doctors, nurses, technicians, food staff, orderlies, bookkeepers, receptionists, and patients arrive at the hospital every day and play out their expected and appropriate roles. Patients talk to doctors about their symptoms; doctors diagnose the problem and suggest a treatment; patients accept the doctor's decision; technicians and nurses administer treatments, food staff prepares and delivers the meals, bookkeepers record the expenses incurred and send a bill to the insurance agencies. In other words, the hospital operates according to organizational structures, roles, and procedures. These structure and channel the activity of the various types of people who work in or are served by the hospital. The structures, roles, and procedures are the medium of their activities, their choices, and their behavior. The players, however, by their actions, reproduce the hospital; their actions make the hospital what it is as a working organization. Were the doctors to turn to preaching, the nurses to turn to playing poker with the patients, the patients to engage in playing musical instruments, and the food staff engage in clothing design, the organization would cease being a hospital.

Nonetheless, within their assigned roles, the hospital staff can either enjoy a culture of interdependent teamwork, or endure a culture of strict hierarchy where doctors rule imperiously over everyone, and all other staff in the pecking order communicate this superior-inferior relationship. Within the former culture, nurses may pass along helpful information about a patient to the attending physician; within the latter culture, nurses would not presume to suggest helpful information to the all-knowing physician.

Schools also exhibit similar characteristics. The school is structured according to different grade levels. Within those grade levels, the daily schedule determines what academic areas will be treated during which time periods of the day. Learners are assigned to various classrooms, working with specific teachers. In each academic area, there is a syllabus that structures what lessons precede others according to a certain logic within the academic disciplines, and creates expectations of student learnings connected to that syllabus. In any given school year, on almost any given day, teachers and students reproduce the structures that channel their activities: they enact the daily and weekly schedule; they focus on the learning activities called for by the syllabus and produce the expected learnings (at least most of the class can more or less perform the expected right answers). The structures are the medium of their activities; the structures are also outcomes of their activities. Nevertheless, within those roles, structures, and procedures, one may find wide differences between schools, due to the levels of freedom and creativity that both students and teachers experience.

Obviously, this analysis leads to a certain pessimism when considering the need for change and improvement in schools. It would appear that organizational structures dominate the free and creative agency of the members. They tend to define reality, to translate "the way things work around here" to a normative assertion that "this is the way things *should* work around here." Thus, human constructs come to be seen as natural, as normal. Deviations are seen as interference with the natural order of things, distortions of the way the work has always been done.

The structure-agency dialectic explains the enormous "drag" of embedded institutional procedures. Changing the structures of schooling requires enormous energies and a sustained effort over several years. That is because structural arrangements have shaped the members' organizational identities, their sense of themselves as competent enactors of their assigned roles. Changing the structures in any significant way (e.g., changing to block scheduling, incorporating constructivist pedagogy in their classrooms) opens the possibility that the teachers might not be able to perform their new roles, that they might be seen as incompetent. Thus, faculty resistance to change can be seen, from a compassionate perspective, as a healthy defense mechanism employed to sustain self-esteem. The structure-agency dialectic also suggests that innovations need to be synchronized with other remaining structures in the school so that the work environment retains some of its former predictability and the fit appears more "natural."

Another aspect of the structure-agency dialectic that human resource leaders must keep in mind concerns a fuller meaning to the term, "agency." Agency is a term used by sociologists in reference to collective human activity in a social setting. It conveys some sense of an individual acting intentionally, with some sense of self. It is often used in contrast to a passive following of instructions given by those in authority, a routine performance of a role that is done automatically and without reflection, a mindless going with the flow. However, agency still means the active performance of a *role* that is defined by the organizational or social situation.

While human resource leaders want teachers and students to observe established organizational procedures in the performance of their roles, they should also think of the teachers' and students' agency in its fuller human dimension. That is, the agency expected of teachers and staff should be enacted in the service of a rich and full human life for all members of the school community, not simply as the rule-governed behavior of a bureaucrat employing technical and political skills to produce higher test scores. Reversing the pessimistic view that structures dominate agency, the human resources of the school should *act on and within the structures* of the school so as to create rich learning opportunities for all the learners in the school. To do this, however, there must be a third element introduced into the structure-agency dialectic, and that is a compelling *vision* of the school, a vision of what it is and what it might become.

The Vision Behind Organizational Leadership

Without denying the duality of structure and agency in organizational life, leaders activate a greater sense of agency among the school's members by promoting a vision of what the school can and should become. Peter Senge (1990) suggested that a tension necessarily exists in organizations between a shared vision and perceived organizational limitations. Senge asserted that this tension can be generative when leaders mobilize the members to use that tension creatively. When the gap between the ideal and the real becomes glaringly significant, the awareness of that gap fuels the commitment of the leader to close that gap.

A vision of where the school is at present and what the school could become suggests that vision enables leaders and members to *see* things more clearly, seeing both the foreground and background and situating the foreground within the background. Vision enables the leader and members to look into the full reality of what stands before them, see it in its complexity and in its human, existential, and moral dimensions as well as its educational and organizational dimensions. This in-sight enables them to grasp both the pragmatic and the deeper, long-term dimensions of situations. Their clarity about the vision enables them to respond to the multidimensional quality of situations, to offer short-term responses that are aligned with longer-term strategies. In other words, repeated everyday problems are frequently symptoms of underlying organizational dysfunctions. Working toward an alignment of those organizational patterns and procedures with a vision of what the school can become enables leaders and members to overcome the oppressive structuration of their communal agency by re-inventing and re-engineering those structures to serve their vision of where the school should be going.

Adding the component of vision to the dynamic between structure and agency enables us to conceive of organizational leadership for human resource development according to a different model, what we might call the Onion Model of Schools (Starratt, 1995). We can visualize a school being made up of layers of intelligible activity (see Figure 4.1).

The outer layer represents the operational level of the school. This is what one sees on walking around the school building on any given day: teachers in front of their classrooms using the blackboard to explain something; students struggling to follow the teacher's explanations; students moving from one classroom to another, banging locker doors, calling out to one another; bulletin boards displaying students' work; teachers in the teachers' lounge discussing the merits of a new textbook.

Between the operational layer and the organizational layers is the all-important layer of school culture, the patterns imbedded across

Figure 4.1 The onion model.

relationships, various rituals, metaphorical ways of talking about the work of students, slanted interpretations about events and happenings around the school. The cultural dynamic subtly shapes the way the school community operates, thinks about itself, articulates and enacts key values and norms. The culture legitimizes "the way things work here." The school culture is the spirit in the air people in the school exhale and inhale, reflected in the ways people in the school treat each other, the way they go about their work, the sensibilities that are respected and expressed in the many interactions among people throughout the school day. The culture enters into the vocabulary and imagery people use to describe significant events and activities in the school. Cultures are open or closed, formal or informal, tightly knit or defined by antagonistic camps, collaborative or individualistic.

Underneath the cultural layer one would find a pattern of organization: a class schedule for each day of the week, distribution of subject matter across the daily class schedule, allocation of approximately twenty-five students to a class, a weekly and monthly calendar of class and special events, the allocation of various support staff doing their respective jobs, a schedule governing the arrival and departure of busses, the vertical and horizontal communication systems, the organization chart representing authority relationships of who reports to whom, and so forth.

Beneath that organizational layer we find the layer of school-wide programs—the various academic disciplines with their scope and sequence for each year, the guidance program, the discipline program, the health program, the athletic program, and school-parent programs. The programs organize the substance of the teachers' and students' work, and constitute, after salaries, the primary cost centers of the budget.

Under that layer is the policy layer. This layer guides the execution of the programs and operations and includes grading and promotion policies; personnel policies for teachers, staff, pupils, and parents; crisis management procedures; student discipline and due process policies. These are the general rules that govern many of the day-to-day decisions made by everyone in the school community. Often, these rules and procedures require fine tuning or complete overhaul because they conflict with other policies, or they are not in alignment with recent changes in school programs, or they are discovered to conflict with the more general goals and objectives of the school.

The next layer involves the articulation of the school's goals and purposes. This layer includes the school mission statement, perhaps a statement of the core values the school espouses, and goals referring to students' intellectual, social and personal development.

Getting closer to the center we find a layer of beliefs and assumptions. Often these are not articulated. Although tacit, they nevertheless exercise an enormous influence over the behavior and routines of people in the school. Often, these unarticulated beliefs and assumptions—what Senge (1990) refers to as "mental models"—are the source of conflicts among teachers, between teachers and parents, and between administrators and teachers. Sometimes these beliefs and assumptions are quite prejudicial to students, leading teachers to categorize students as problems, as messes to be fixed. The assumption might be that students are expected to be passive recipients of the knowledge the teacher and the textbook deliver, or that the grading system should reflect the "normal curve" of intelligence. On the other hand, those beliefs may be more student-friendly, focusing on the enormous potential of the learners, believing that the work of teaching at its best is creative and life-giving. In any event, this is the level where the vision will be articulated, since vision is very much an expression of beliefs and assumptions about the nature of the work the school is engaged in presently, and about the direction the school should be moving in.

At the core of the onion, often flowing into the unarticulated beliefs and assumptions, are the myths and meanings by which people make sense out of their lives. By labeling them myths, I do not imply that they are fairy-tale fantasies fed by fears, desires, and superstitions. Rather, these myths are stories whose symbolism enables us to define, value, judge human striving, and place ourselves in an identifiable order of things. This core is almost beyond articulation. It includes myths of heroism, human destiny, courage, and the sacred nature of all life; myths about society's relationship to nature, about values underlying the nation's identity, about those values central to the essence of humanity. Those myths—often embodied in story, poetry, highly symbolic literature, sacred texts—shape people's convictions, attitudes, and beliefs about most things. It is in that core of myth, meaning, and belief that leaders find the foundation for their vision of what the school can and should become: the greenhouse for cultivating the enormous potential in human beings, the soil for growing the nation's artists, heroes, craftspersons, peacemakers, statespersons, scientists, negotiators, comedians, trailblazers, inventors, composers, diplomats, architects, healers, prophets, educators, as well as the loving mothers and fathers of future generations of healthy and fulfilled human beings.

The articulation of the vision is crucial. Without a communal vision of who they are and where they want to go, the school functions as a shopping mall, with each classroom reflecting the idiosyncratic preferences of each teacher (Powell, Farrar, & Cohen, 1985). Absent a communal vision, a fluctuating or temporary vision is inevitably imposed from outside. Indeed, state departments of education, pressured by political and corporate leaders with a one-dimensional view of schooling, have been quite willing to step in and impose their view of schooling. Currently in many countries, government policies imply that schools are primarily instruments of the market economy. Policies focus on teaching those skills and understandings that will prepare the nation's workforce to be competitive in the international competition for market share and compliant consumers of the goods the market produces. On the other hand, a vision of schooling developed and endorsed by the school staff can serve as a framework for interpreting the limits of such a one-dimensional viewpoint of a mass administered, mass producing, and mass consuming society and balancing that viewpoint with a view of human and social flourishing in a polity and an economy that honors human creativity and human service within a sustainable local and global environment.

Often leaders have to take the initiative and put forth a vision statement. That initial statement provides the rest of the community something to consider, but not necessarily to endorse. Individually and in teams of parents, teachers, and school committees, they should be encouraged to come up with their vision—not only of where they are now, but a vision of who and what they might become—a vision of new understandings of their work, a vision of where they want to go with the students.

The leaders' work is not completed when the school community has articulated its communal vision. Indeed, it has just begun. The vision must become embodied in the other layers of the school organization. The onion must be energized by its core. The difficulty experienced by many educators is that they function in schools that, for all intents and purposes, have no center, no articulated vision, mission, or sense of purpose, other than the daily delivery of programs governed by schedules and operating procedures (see Figure 4.2).

Figure 4.2

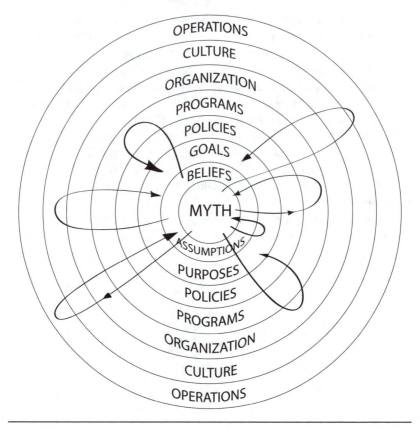

Figure 4.3

In contrast, Figure 4.3 suggests a school in which the outer layers reflect those core beliefs, values, and meanings. The articulation of a vision enables those school communities to intentionally evaluate their school culture and the values embedded and expressed in their habitual ways they treat each other. The vision is the compass for guiding the school's journey. The culture refers to the spirit in which the voyagers carry out the work of the journey. The vision becomes activated and operationalized by means of the programs and structural organization of the school. Those programs and the organizational structures and routines need to be energized by and reflect the vision, rather than simply existing in some neutral self-justifying space, or worse, as opponents of the vision. The vision statement does not have a sustainable impact on student learning unless it is institutionalized in all the various layers of school life. Schools that fail to confront the disconnect between their organizational structures and their vision remain dysfunctional.

The Integration of Leadership Work and Management Work

The work of bringing the vision to life within the other layers of the school organization involves two sides of the work of the human resource developer. Figure 4.4 attempts to visualize the division of labor, so to speak, between the leadership work of the human resource developer and the management work.

Much of the leader's work involves working with the core of the onion model, working with the staff to spell out the vision clearly and in terms that the whole staff can endorse. Bringing educators together to construct the vision is time-consuming and disciplined, reflective work. Teachers are not accustomed to the conceptual work of trying to capture something grand and ennobling in words that reflect their deepest beliefs as educators. Their daily activities force them to attend to many practical details of managing a classroom of learners who bring a wide diversity of interests, talents, challenges, and backgrounds. They are caught up in the immediacy of their work; they are seldom asked or given the time to reflect at this level.

This task asks them to respond to the questions: Who are we? How would others describe us and our work together? How would we like others to describe our work together? The questions imply considering not only the individual sense of themselves, but also their sense of themselves as a community made up of educators, learners, and support staff. It asks them to look at their collective talents, interests, backgrounds, and challenges— to look at themselves and what their work together means to them. That means acknowledging not only their shortcomings but also their achievements; acknowledging their dreams as well as their defeats, acknowledging the good they do, as well as the good they leave undone. The vision also demands that they look at the larger social and political purposes the school serves on behalf of the civic community. The civic values of freedom, democratic participation and promoting the common good necessarily enter into the articulation of the vision.

In this work the use of metaphor and imagery can be quite helpful in expressing the ambiguities they feel caught up in. We are wounded healers. We are haphazard heroes. We are angels flying too close to the ground. We are on a journey with an incomplete map. We are prisoners of hope. We are midwives to a generational birthing process that has no sure conclusion. We are wisdom figures uncertain of our wisdom. We are teachers being taught by our pupils. We hold the future in our trembling hands every day. We are prisoners of a broken system who refuse to surrender. Too often educators succumb to a toxic cynicism that disavows any idealism. The absence of any communal dreams, however, simply justifies the

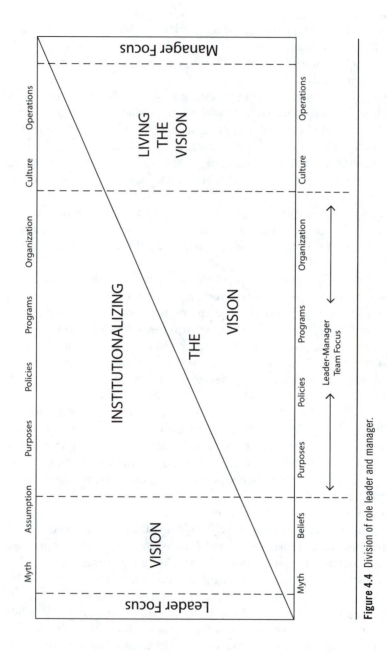

Figure 4.4 Division of role leader and manager.

dysfunctional status quo. The problem is not with ideals and dreams of a better life; it is the absence of the will and the courage to start with small success; it is the absence of belief in our own potential for greatness.

With some sense of the potential inherent in their collective membership and in their work together, as well as the challenges they each face individually and they all face collectively, they then are asked: What is it we want to become as an educating community? What do we want to look like in five to seven years? How would we like others describe us and our work then? Responses to these questions should take into account the present limitations and obstacles they face, not as insuperable limitations but as challenges to be overcome, or diminished. The responses should express their deep beliefs and convictions about their own human potential and that of the students, as well as the potential of the various curriculums of the school to contribute to the fuller human growth of the students.

In some situations, the vision will already exist and may need but a renewed commitment. In other situations, the leaders may be faced with a complete absence of vision. In this case the building of a vision will take an extended period of time. The leader may have to be satisfied initially with building a minimal level of trust so that teachers might share life stories that reveal some of their mythic understandings of important aspects of their beliefs. This work easily spills over into the work of renewing the school culture, bringing people to explicitly assess how they treat one another, what values are implicit in the customs and routines of everyday life in the school. This work does not preclude the leader's involvement with improving the organizational policies and programs of the school. Sometimes visions have to be built out of a collective attending to the more mundane and practical aspects of school life. As people discuss reasons for making change in the more external layers of the school, disagreements about the values and assumptions behind the changes may surface. What the leaders will be seeking is a growing consistency across layers of the organization such that important values embedded in policies are also reflected in the way programs are resourced and implemented.

The second side of the work involves attention to managing the specifics. The human resource developer will attend to the various ways the human resources are in fact carrying out the daily operations of the school. In that capacity, the human resource leader will engage in the more technical functions of monitoring, motivating, problem solving, program development, coordinating, increasing communication flow, arbitrating conflicts, and so forth. In all of these managerial tasks, however, the human resource administrator will remember the vision, will use the technical work to remind the members of the deeper significance of what they are doing, will raise questions that tie practical decisions to the vision, will use the vision to question the interpretation of a discipline or grading policy.

As Figure 4.4 indicates, with the vision at least partially in place, the focus of the human resource leader will tend to concentrate on the middle organizational layers of the school, blending leadership tasks with managerial tasks. Nevertheless, attending to vision as it is expressed at every level of the organization will be an underlying concern, even attending to celebrating the vision within the operational level through various school rituals during the year.

Summary

The Onion Model of the school as an organization helps us understand the importance of the organizational dimension of human resource leadership, calling our attention to the necessary involvement of the human resources of the school around purposes, policies, programs, organization, culture, and operations. It suggests that the tensions between personal fulfillment and organizational demands can be at least partially resolved as the school staff find increasing fulfillment in collectively working toward the realization of a vision of themselves and their work that is deeply satisfying. It also enables us to recognize that organizational structures need not so routinize the agency of the members that their own initiative and creativity is stifled. Rather, teachers, students, and staff can indeed be happy to reproduce the structures of their schools when those structures are enabling them to realize their vision of themselves and their work as holding enormous significance. This does not mean that structures will never get in the way. With a clear vision of what they are supposed to be doing, however, the members will address cultural and structural obstacles as human constructs meant to enable rather than hinder the vision (Hoy & Sweetland, 2001). The further refinement of organizational structures to serve the vision better becomes a work combining the joint talents of leader and manager. Working on those refinements will be seen as part of the learning process of the learning community.

From a more exclusive focus on the technical demands of human resource leadership, we can also see how the onion model provides a model for the human resource developer. The technical work of recruiting, hiring, induction, mentoring, evaluating, continuing professional development, negotiating working conditions, and even the process of contract termination is best served by a vision of the significance of the human as the greatest resource any community could ask for. That vision of the human grounds and guides the purposes and goals of all human resource leadership.

With this large perspective on the organizational context of human resource leadership, we can proceed to a further consideration of another dimension of human resource administration, the political dimension. We should remind ourselves, that these "dimensions" are not separate, compartmentalized silos. Rather, they illuminate and interpenetrate one another. While separated for conceptual analysis, we realize that the political dimension is situated within the organizational life of the school, with its own particular purposes, policies, and programs that nevertheless should be tied to the vision of the school.

CHAPTER 5

The Politics of Human Resource Development

Introduction: The Politics of Sociality

Modern biology, chemistry, physics, cosmology and environmental sciences, as well as the human and social sciences all reveal that *relationality* constitutes the essence of everything. Nothing exists in isolation. All parts of nature are connected to other parts; world-wide concern for sustainable natural systems presently occupies scientists, citizens and their governments. El Nino Pacific currents and temperatures affect rainfall and climatic variations across all of North America. All humans are connected through their genetic inheritance with their ancestors, both human and non-human. All humans are connected with other humans through the cultural communities that contribute to their identity. Human beings are persons in so far as they are engaged in relationships. When there is no "other" for me, I am a non person. One person is no person. We live together or we do not live at all. We must dispel the notion that we live tangentially, each one of us occupying separate space. Rather, we live in a human field where the past echoes and fingerprints the present, and the announcement over the Internet of an invention in Tibet catches the attention ten minutes later of an engineer in Mexico. The filling out of our soul, the becoming of a richer more complex person happens with and because of other persons. We come alive when we share our space with another and when an other shares their space with us.

Who we are is largely constituted by the people and the ideas we have taken inside and who have taken us inside. Who we will become will largely be constituted by those people and ideas we will take inside and who will take us inside. Ideas are the world in words and images that we listen to and share in order to understand and engage the world as our gift and our responsibility. Through ideas we assert our relationship to the world as its children and its stewards, and the world's relationship to ourselves as both gift and responsibility. Other persons constitute our responsibility and our gift as much as we constitute their responsibility and their gift.

In schools we live everyday with other person—teachers, administrators, support staff, and children. They are our gift and our responsibility— our gift in their potential to enrich us by their spirit, their beauty, their talents, their difference; our responsibility in their need to be protected, respected, affirmed, and loved. We are likewise their gift and responsibility—their gift in our potential to enrich them by our spirit, our beauty, our talent, and our difference; their responsibility in our need to be protected, respected, affirmed, and loved.

In our work, we co-construct and share our world through words and images with younger humans so that they as individuals and as a whole generation might take the world inside them as their gift and responsibility and be taken inside by the world as their home. In that work, we reveal how the world is our gift and responsibility.

Sometimes, however, we teach the world as abstract formulas, definitions, as words and images to be memorized as answers to test questions, as pages in a book to be covered, as knowledge disconnected from responsibility and wonder and self-implication and challenge. Sometimes we avoid looking into our pupils' eyes, looking into their lives, looking into their fears, insecurities, struggles, looking for the talent and curiosity and self-journey they aspire to. We fail to see them as gift and responsibility, and fail to allow ourselves to be gift and responsibility to them. That failure dissipates the enormous human energy that could flow between them and us, and among them and the world in a learning process that could be full of wonder, of surprise, of self-knowledge and self-engagement. We see the same with our faculty colleagues: impersonality and surface civility masks our continuous distancing ourselves from them, thereby denying them as gifts and denying any responsibility to befriend them and to support them in their struggles.

Every day we engage either in the politics of empowerment or the politics of disempowerment in the way we exercise our basic relationality to one another, to the world, and to the learning process. Our choices carry power, power for gifting, or power for withholding the gift. That political agency empowers or disempowers us as well, grows our relationality or diminishes it, and thereby grows us as persons and grows other people, or withers us and stifles other people. One might say that all our interpersonal agency—whether as spouses, as parents, as brothers and sisters, as neighbors, as colleagues in a common enterprise—is political: political insofar as it empowers or disempowers.

Disclaimers of such either-or choices in a retreat to simple interpersonal neutrality in our relationships won't stand up. We either give of ourselves and thereby assert our responsibility for the other, or we deny such giving as well as the inherent responsibility for giving. From this perspective, the human journey, which is inherently relational, is inherently political, and inherently moral, weighted with the power to create or diminish goodness in all the circumstances of our lives.

For those who lead in the work of education—understanding the work of education as human development—the message is clear. You cultivate a culture of empowerment, or you tolerate or support a culture of disempowerment; you cultivate a culture of community or you tolerate or support a culture of isolated individuals whose social contract at best is not to interfere with each other's right to self-seeking and self-promoting in a world that exists for human exploitation and consumption and in an educational process that seeks to dominate in a competition for scarce resources and limited spaces at the top.

The politics of a self-governing community is the answer to such a dehumanizing political social contract. The guiding principle of such a self-governing community is honoring the gift of the other and taking responsibility for gifting the other with our support and care. The praxis of such a self-governing community is to establish and follow a stable series of intentional processes for negotiating our relationality and negotiating an equitable share of common resources, such negotiations always to be governed by a care for the human person. With the ontology of relationality as its foundation, we turn now to the explicit realm of the political in the work of leading human resource development in education.

This chapter examines human resource development within a commitment to democracy as an ideal and as a process. Some contradictions between the mission of the school and the way schools operate in the present political climate of the state and nation will be highlighted along with the implications of the current policy assumptions about learning. The chapter will move on to explore the contentious and adversarial political environment internal to school systems, followed by a discussion of political leadership as coalition building, the politics of community, and embedding the value commitments behind a democratic governance in the human resource system itself.

As has been emphasized in earlier chapters, human resource development in education involves all administrators and teachers in the school and the school system. All of them have to guide, coordinate, manage, monitor, and, in one way or another, lead the human resources within the organizational unit they administer. Their work necessarily involves them as agents of the politics of the school system, as participants in the politics of the local school, and as coordinators and managers of the internal politics of their administrative unit.

Earlier chapters also embrace the theme that human resource administration not only concerns itself with the professional staff and the support staff of the school, but also with the learners, for they, too, are essential human resources in carrying out the work of the school. The work of the learners is the core work of the school. Human resource development on behalf of the teaching faculty has to serve the learning needs of the learners. Thus, when considering the political dimension of human resource leadership, we begin with the learners and take into consideration the content and the process of their learning from a political perspective, namely their learning of the elements of citizen participation in their classrooms, on the school playground, in the cafeteria and corridors, and their roles as citizens in a democratic society. They learn the politics of democracy, not only in the lunchroom and the playground, not only in co-curricular activities, but, as was emphasized in chapter 2, even while learning the academic curriculum (Barton & Levstik, 2004).

The Democratic Ideal

An important dimension of human resource leadership within a public, or state school system is that it operates in a public institution, an institution serving state and national purposes. A specific purpose of schools anywhere is to educate the young. Education in the United States and other democracies, however, is not an education within a dictatorship, nor within a monarchy; it is an education within a democracy, intended to prepare citizens to participate in its democratic way of life.

There are different versions of democracy. Democracy in Switzerland differs from democracy in Sweden, or in Italy, or in Japan. Human resource development in schools in the United States will practice and serve its own unique democratic character.

In the United States since September 11, 2001, and its aftermath, there has been a deepening awareness of democracy as a cherished and threatened heritage. While this has led some to a simplistic, defensive, almost isolationist view of U.S. democracy as threatened on all sides by a hostile coalition of nondemocratic forces, it has led others to a more thoughtful appreciation of what it takes to make a democracy work, beyond a strong military and police force dedicated to its defense. This is not the place to debate national and international policies to strengthen the democratic tradition and spirit in the United States. It is the place, however, to deliberate the connection of our political heritage, our form of democracy—its core ideas and values—to the practice of human resource leadership in all schools.

The democratic character of the lives and work of educators in schools is not something to be simply assumed, as though it is absorbed by osmosis by living in a democratic country. Rather, it is something that has to be nourished, affirmed, and cultivated especially in the work of schools (Barber, 1998; Dewey, 1916; Furman & Starratt, 2002; Horn, 2008; Jenlink, 2008; Oakes, Quartz, Ryan, & Lipton, 2000; Starratt, 2001, 2008). Schools are meant to be a primary place where democracy is learned and taught for every succeeding generation of citizens. The democratic nature of the work of teaching and learning should model and articulate the character of democratic citizenship and public service.

From this standpoint, human resource leadership in education should be seen to support the mission of the schools to prepare citizens to participate in the democratic way of life of its country. Clearly, this participation requires the basic ability to read and to communicate, to understand the basics of physical, social, and cultural health, to be sufficiently proficient in mathematics and the sciences to participate in the workforce and to vote on public policy, to know the history of their country and of the countries of the world. That involves a study of peoples' struggles for human and civil liberties that history reveals. Participation in the democratic way of life of their country also assumes that these young citizens know their own civil and human rights and responsibilities and have learned them through actual experience and by studying historical exemplars (Broudy, Smith, & Burnett 1964).

More specifically, they need to learn that democracy is a form of associated living based on common experiences of sociality among citizens (Dewey, 1916; Barber, 1998; Block, 2002). Without that social foundation, the politics of democracy can degenerate into various forms of self-interested individualism, claiming rights and privileges *against and in spite of* the civil community. Thus, education is supposed to prepare youth to weigh personal interests against the common needs of the community for security, order, and justice. Their education is supposed to help them participate in the use, maintenance, and sharing of public resources like water, air, information, transportation systems, and medical care. To be sure, a significant part of that participation will involve their adult work, both for their own sustenance and for the health of the economic condition of the nation and state; thus their education is also meant to prepare them with the basic skills and understandings necessary to train for careers after they graduate from secondary school.

Beyond that, however, their education is supposed to prepare them to engage in the free market of ideas, in the development of creative cultural expression, in debates over acceptable and desirable public policies for their local neighborhoods, their regions, and the network of nations around the globe. It is supposed to help them learn when they must insist on rights over responsibilities under some circumstances and when, under others, they must insist on responsibilities to the community over individual rights. It is supposed to teach them what protections they enjoy under the law, and what obligations they carry under the law. Beyond that, their education is supposed to engage them in the basic lessons of sociality, of respect for all persons, of the need to care for those less fortunate than themselves, of their basic human ties of brotherhood and sisterhood with everyone, no matter how different they appear in color, dress, age, religion, or social status. A moment's reflection on these democratic public purposes of schools will begin to generate multiple implications for the human resource administration of schools: the kind of values to look for in people applying for teaching positions; the way rules and guidelines for the workplace are developed; the way teacher evaluation systems are formed and administered; and the shaping of professional development opportunities.

Conflicts Over Interpretations of the Democratic Ideal

More recently in the United States and elsewhere, some have proposed that schools be run like business corporations. This would involve substituting a dominant economic rationale (and a survival of the fittest one, at that) for the basic social purposes of the schools. That rationale starts by equating learning and the acquisition of knowledge with the work of mastering the right answers on standardized academic tests—tests, by the way, that do not assess these students' readiness for participation in a democratic society. For individual students, those test scores would be equated with "academic achievement," the "products" their labor in schools was supposed to produce. Test scores constitute the coinage of the realm of schooling. Those who produced good scores would be reward with acceptance at better colleges and better jobs; those who did not produce good scores would be denied promotion and diplomas, and supposedly relegated to minimum-wage jobs and the rolls of welfare. Supposedly, fear of such a fate would spur previously unmotivated students to work harder for acceptable grades.

For schools, their accumulated test scores would reveal their "productivity." In a free market for schooling, those schools that produced higher test scores would survive, because they would be the ones parents would choose. Of course, colleges and universities would tend to prefer candidates from those "high performing" schools. The opposite would hold true for schools with low test scores. They would be closed or put into receivership on the grounds that they were wasting taxpayers' money. Furthermore, it is assumed that no one would want to send their children there. What is not admitted is that most of these schools cannot be closed because there is no place to send the low performing children.

The complex problems in a globalizing world, however, are not simply economic. They are also political, cultural, and environmental. Schools will need to prepare young people for an international democratic way of life in much the same fashion as they have tried to prepare them for a national and local democratic way of life.

The pressures of globalization are already present in the schools of industrialized nations with increasing cultural diversity within the student body. Schools are the places where young people are learning to live with people quite different from themselves. All countries are facing the crossing of their national borders by refugees and immigrants, as well as by banks, corporations, universities, manufactured goods, service providers, and popular media. To think that the work of schools is exclusively to prepare students for exams in mathematics and literacy and ignore the many socializing lessons schools have always taught is to be blind to the realities faced even within the business world, and certainly in the political and cultural worlds of today.

Schools as the State in Action

When educators arrive at school every day, they represent the state. They represent the ideals the state stands for. Schools are chartered by the state to serve the interests of the people who, under the Constitution, continually enact the state. Teachers are the state educating its citizens. Those public servants who work in schools are there as citizens who are providing a public service to fellow citizens, namely, providing the opportunity to learn about the natural, cultural, economic, and political worlds they inhabit. Educators are there to see that, through their work with the young, democracy works; they are there to further the enlightened democracy of the people.

In their work, they educate youth in the values and ideals behind the state, and educate them in the skills and understandings that help democracy work, so that they may themselves eventually become the state in their common and collective activity. This is a cause worth giving a life to, a cause that stretches educators' imaginations beyond the satisfactions of their personal desires and dreams of happiness, toward participation in something immensely significant and valuable, not simply for the country, but for the rest of mankind.

Approaching the more pragmatic side of the work, educators with human resource responsibilities have to observe the public responsibilities expected of them to follow the regulations and policies of the district school board or committee, of the state department of education, and of the state and federal legislation around equity issues, inclusion issues, opportunity-to-learn issues, curriculum guidelines, contractual issues, security and protection issues, parental concerns, and so forth. In other words, their work as public servants requires them to be responsive to the governing bodies and their demands; they work for those governing bodies as well as for individual citizens involved in the school. Sometimes they have to represent the concerns of the citizens to the governing bodies, and sometimes represent the concerns of the governing bodies to the citizens of the school.

The core of their work, however, is to see that the school is a democratic place, a place where the ideals of democracy are taught, honored, and striven for. That means encouraging the basic sociality upon which all other aspects of democracy rests (Dewey, 1916). That basic sociality implies a respecting of persons, a caring for persons, a sharing of school resources fairly, a working at communal self-governing at all times, and at forming those explicit agreements that will help the community carry on its work of learning. Hence, teachers and staff should help to shape the rules they all have to live by. Through their collective deliberation, they should declare the core values the school will actively promote. Through their collective deliberation, they should affirm the work that will be required of everyone, and the criteria for assessing the quality of that work. These deliberations should be carried out in a coherent interface with school district policies.

Within that spirit, human resource leadership will involve parents with children in the school in shaping appropriate parts of the human resource system, especially those involving their own participation in the education of their children and their participation in school activities. Likewise, students should be involved as much as possible and appropriate in their own self-governance through the use of student arbitration teams, big brother and sister teams, peer tutoring, student council, student newspaper, student store, student fairs, and so forth. Human resource leadership should thereby promote a form of self-governance—obviously, within the boundaries set by the state and district school committee.

Democratic Politics and Human Resource Development

Politics is often considered a dirty word. The negative connotations of the word imply deals made behind closed doors, playing favorites, "pork" in legislation that secures funding for questionable local projects that provides jobs and "sweetheart" contracts for political supporters and cronies, appointments of people with questionable qualifications to positions in government through patronage and personal friendships, compromising one's stand on stated public principles to gain political advantage.

While everyone can point to one or more examples of the above negative stereotypes, another, more positive view of politics is possible, such as the following:

- Politics is derived from the term *polity*, which refers to the public life of a community. Politics is that form of group action that is involved with changing, supporting, ameliorating some aspect of the public life of a community.
- Politics is a form of influencing others to do something in the public sphere that they might not spontaneously choose to do.
- Politics involves convincing others to do in the public sphere something they were previously uninformed about.
- Politics involves motivating others to join with a group or a coalition of groups to achieve some larger public goal.

This view of politics is positive in the sense that the goals may be highly contested, but the process involves people coming together, acting together to bring about what they conceive to be a common benefit. Understood in this way, politics can be seen as a much more commonplace activity that takes place in families, neighborhoods, churches, neighborhood coffee shops, schools, corporations. It is in this more commonplace sense that we wish to look at the political side of human resource leadership. For now we want to concentrate on the internal political environment of the school.

From one perspective, the internal politics within the school system is a way of carrying out the internal governance of the system. Often this is done through a system of standing committees, supplemented by ad hoc committees and project teams set up to deal with specific areas and problems in those areas. These committees both design policies that guide the internal work of the school, as well as recommend implementation strategies and problem solutions under those guidelines. Those committees are political in the sense that it is their job to be influenced, convinced and motivated by the ideas and suggestions made to them by the school community; in turn, they influence, convince and motivate the school community to follow their policies and recommendations.

Administrators with human resource responsibilities should see that the membership on those committees represent a variety of perspectives and should be made up of representatives of those to be most affected by the policies and decisions those committees hand down. Each member of those committees—be they teachers, students, parents, or administrators—should have some sense that they are citizens of the school community and that their committee is there to serve the common good of the school community.

Politics as the Expression and Negotiation of Conflict

Another perspective on the internal politics of the school sees political work involving the resolution of conflicts over scarce or limited resources, over values, over policy implementation, over status, over interpretation of rules. Within the human resource arena, these conflicts frequently involve specific issues such as:

- disagreements over administrative versus professional prerogatives;
- disputes over salaries and benefits, or contractual obligations;
- disagreements and resentments among teachers and between departments over the allocation of resources;
- conflicts between parents and teachers over the behavior and achievement of students;
- conflicts over race, diversity, gender, status.

Politics as Coalition Building

Politics is about power and influence. Some engage in politics in order to hold power *over* others, to control them, to force them to do or accept what those in power want. However, power over people depends on them allowing others to exercise that power. When people decide that those in power have lost their legitimacy and subsequently withdraw their acceptance of those in power, then it is only a matter of time before the Berlin walls come down, before those in power are impeached or replaced.

Another interpretation of power and influence places the emphasis on power *with* others. This is the power of people who agree to move in a certain direction, to espouse a cause, to seek a common goal. It is the power of individual people united behind an idea, a principle, a purpose, often embodied in a very specific goal. There will be leaders who mobilize that power. These leaders do not have power over the people; they generate power *with* people. The coalition leader reflects a keen perception of how the various interests and needs of each group intersect and overlap around a common value or concern. The coalition leader quickly identifies the leaders in each group, communicates with them about the common value or concern they share with the other groups, and persuades them of the benefits of collaborating with other groups. Furthermore, that leader perceives the special strengths, abilities, and resources within each group that will complement the different strengths, abilities, and resources of other groups. As the groups come together, the coalition leader helps to coordinate the particular contributions of each group into a workable plan with specific deadlines and targets that will lead the coalition forward toward the goal.

The power of coalitions comes not only from their united activity; it comes from the powerful ideas, purposes, and goals that energize that activity (Burns, 1978). This is the kind of power that a democratic educational politics espouses. It is usually generated by a bringing together of various individuals and groups who have different interests and desires (parents, teachers, custodians, coaches, counselors, students, and administrators) around a compelling common effort, a purpose that touches upon their common humanity, their common needs, their common aspirations for achieving something out of the ordinary (Eisenstadt, 1968).

The ideal or high purpose, however, cannot by itself make such a coalition effective. The members of the coalition have to be empowered to contribute to the work. An important part of the politics of coalitions is the politics of empowerment. This results not from leaders giving power to the participants, but from encouraging them to find the power in themselves and in their collective participation in the work (Blasé & Blasé, 2001). This encouragement of initiative on the part of the coalition members has to be grounded in trust, an all pervasive quality found in successful efforts at school renewal (Bryk & Schneider, 2002: Hoy, 2002). Grounded in trust that all the participants in the coalition will abide by their agreements, this collective participation encourages a growing sense of efficacy of all the members of the coalition—the sense that, when they put their collective heads and hearts behind the effort, they can always find a way to overcome any problem the work throws up at them (Bandura, 1997).

That sense of efficacy, in turn, involves them in taking responsibility for carrying out the work. It is their work, and they can find pride in doing it well; they can take the credit for moving toward their ambitious goals. With that sense of owning the work and the results of their work together, the various members of the coalition find their own form of human fulfillment. Involvement of a coalition of teachers, students, parents, and system administrators in comprehensive school improvement can generate a shared fulfillment: fulfillment for teachers and administrators in seeing learners becoming enthusiastically engaged in the activity of learning through the stimulation of their teaching; fulfillment for students in encountering the natural and cultural world in its fascinating complexity, and thereby coming to embrace their membership in those worlds; fulfillment of administrators who see the results of their careful and inventive redesign and management of the organizational structures, policies, and processes of the school in the more effective work of students and teachers; fulfillment of parents who see their children's minds and hearts expanding toward a more mature humanity filled with greater promise.

The Response of Realpolitik

This treatment of the politics of democracy may sound too sugar-coated, too idealistic, disconnected from the harsher tones of the politics of reality. Realpolitik assumes that the reality of human relations and power in society and between societies is motivated primarily, if not exclusively by self-interest, and a narrow form of self-interest at that. Thus, realpolitik is always a matter of power in conflict with power: the power of one individual against the power of another individual; the power of one group against the power of another group; the power of one nation in competition with the power of another nation. This theory of politics will grudgingly admit that from time to time, coalitions of these narrow, self-interested groups or nations will come together to unite their collective power in opposition to another powerful group of nations. Those coalitions will last as long as the disparate members of the coalition perceive that their self-interests are served by the coalition. Over time, coalitions break apart, sometimes reshaping allegiances with some former enemies against former partners. Proponents of realpolitik tend to view the espousal of ideals and common human values by these coalitions as simply a rhetorical ploy intended to dignify or justify what in itself is a game of raw power, a game of winners and losers in the unending competition for advantage over others.

Realpolitik becomes a self-fulfilling prophecy. Two sides who espouse the theory of realpolitik can never unite as a large community of humans involved in a common destiny. They are doomed at the outset, by definition, to a never-ending history of competition and mutual antagonism, always cynical about each other's intentions, with no chance of moving to a more mature sense of mutual responsibility for their common human destiny. What they claim as political reality is what they have constructed, not what political reality might become. They repeat the self-centered nature of child-play on a more lethal scale. They have yet to learn a more mature form of politics.

An appeal to build coalitions that serve democratic ideals is not a Pollyannaish fantasy. It is a call to be true to the best part of our national heritage, as well as to our particular human destiny. It is not an attempt to wipe out diversity and plurality, to negate otherness, to impose a simplistic homogeneity on groups whose differences run deep. The national motto, *e pluribus unum*, implies neither an anarchic plurality nor a homogeneous uniformity. Rather, it implies the continuous process of forming a common ground among diverse people who can celebrate both their diversity and their common citizenship in larger community, a community that is not diminished but enriched by its diversity.

From Coalitions to Community

Through continuously encouraging, supporting, and coordinating the work of coalitions, human resource administrators can begin to develop a deeper, more mature political culture, namely, a culture of community. The culture of community carries the politics of negotiation among various self-interested groups toward a deeper politics—the binding in mutuality with all members of the school community, reflecting the metaphor of a large family. The one-dimensional bargaining among participants for a larger share of resources becomes tempered by a deeper felt responsibility of each to all. The lines between the self-interest of individuals and groups become more porous as a larger group identity becomes embraced. The school members more often begin to speak in terms of "we" (Swanson, Meehan, & Hubbard, 1995; Comer, Haynes, Joyner, & Ben-Avie, 1996).

Belonging to a community brings with it a strengthened individual identity. A healthy individual needs a community, and a healthy community needs unique individuals to contribute to its vitality. Clearly in line with Dewey's rejection of the dualism of individual versus community where the two are seen as opposed to or canceling out each other (Dewey, 1916), this view of community affirms that both the individual and community are necessary for the full life of each other (Becker, 1967). The tensions between individual freedom and the common good of the community are essential to the growth of both. Freedom expands in communities where the common good of all is promoted; the common good benefits from the creativity, inventiveness, and energy of free individuals who thereby expand the community's horizons, enrich the community's cultural complexity, and create new opportunities for others in the community.

Oakes (Oakes & Quartz, 1995; Oakes, Quartz, Ryan, & Lipton, 2000) argues for leadership of this gradual transformation of the coalition into a community and sees it explicitly as a political process, just as unequal relationships of power to be found in most schools are also a result of a political process. As Beck, Giddens, and Lash (1994) observe, however, community can be more than or less than a group of citizens sharing decision-making power. A baseball team may exhibit the closeness of a community but not conduct its business democratically. The common good that ties the team together is winning the game, not shared decision making and civil rights. However, a school that promotes common values, a sense of family, mutual caring, *and* decision making around its common good may be said to represent a community that deserves the label, democratic community.

To place the responsibility for engaging in the politics of democratic community squarely on the shoulders of administrators and teachers whose responsibilities include the cultivation of human resources will seem to some a daring challenge. I suspect it will appear a daring challenge because of the unspoken acceptance by administrators and teachers of the politics of realpolitik. But acceptance of this theory has already produced a self-fulfilling prophecy. Schools tend to reflect the politics of self-interest: teachers against administrator's power; students resisting the power of the teachers; parents resenting the power of teachers and administrators over their children; the school board resisting the power of the teachers' bargaining association; the business community resisting the power of public institutions and the tax burdens and regulations they impose.

To suggest that human resource development functions according to democratic politics assumes that every week the daily affairs of the schools will have to be negotiated—not because schools are composed of antagonistic, narrowly self-interested groups, but because schools are composed of capable, inventive, and efficacious people. In such an environment, negotiations are not about seeking advantage of one group over another. Rather, they are seeking to negotiate differences of opinion on how best to get the work done. By sharing various opinions, ideas get explored, trial-and-error learning can occur, and mutual reinforcement of practical breakthroughs in the teaching and learning process occurs.

The job of the human resource leader is constantly to remind the human beings in the school that their work is potentially exciting, fulfilling, and dramatic work. That work issues in the slow progress of learning that cumulatively, over time, enables young people to define themselves in relationship to the worlds they are studying. It helps them to ask questions of themselves and ask questions about how the world might work better than it does. Their daily advances in learning sows the seeds of larger insights, inventiveness, new questions, new dreams of what might be. That learning is the energy that will fuel their engagement with a future filled with possibilities as well as dangers, a future that challenges all nations and peoples to redefine themselves and their destinies. By calling attention to the dramatic possibilities and satisfactions of the work of teaching and learning, the human resource leader keeps the various coalitions of the school community focused around learning issues, helps them generate various responses to learning challenges that different learners encounter, supports their inquiries and pragmatic testing of responses. Human resource leaders will constantly urge all the groups in the school to find in the work some of their deepest human satisfactions and their deepest source of value. There will be politics aplenty, but it will be a politics of people negotiating with one another for a more fulfilling enactment of the work of learning. In the work they will find their greatest self-interest, the goal of engaging in something of extraordinary value that confers on them a dignity well beyond anything that a huge salary could confer.

Perhaps educators can measure their disbelief in this kind of politics by the depth of their acceptance of the poverty and cynicism we experience in the other kind of politics. In arguing for the politics of democratic education, I am not discounting the reality of realpolitik. The attitudes and beliefs that support such an approach to politics will not evanesce by our wishing it. The strength of those attitudes and beliefs, however, will weaken over time through the experience of the more humanly fulfilling engagement in a democratic politics around authentic learning, and increasing transparency and trust in our working relationships. By appealing to the intrinsic value of the work, and by empowering both students and teachers to engage that work efficaciously, leaders in schools will gradually weaken the other interpretation of self-interest that pits groups against one another.

Realpolitik is too deeply entrenched within our history of individualism and capitalist economics to expect its demise. It has infected our national politics for centuries, compromising and distorting our democratic ideals. The issue is whether one form of politics or the other will dominate our social lives. For educators seeking to serve the full humanity of both teachers and learners, the choice seems obvious. It will mean an explicit assessment and articulation of the political landscape in schools and school districts, encouraging discussions on the merits and deficits of each form of politics. Initial research on the politics of trust (Bryk & Schneider, 2002; Hoy, 2002), provides initial indications that schools that build a strong foundation of trust between various groups within the school are the most successful academically. Could it be that schools that emphasize the basic sociality upon which democracy flourishes can point the way for national realignment of the way we treat each other in schools? Perhaps the words of the Reverend Martin Luther King (1967) can continue to provide a compass for this journey.

Dr. Martin Luther King on the Relationship of Power and Love

Power, properly understood, is the ability to achieve purpose. It is the strength required to bring about social, political, or economic changes. In this sense power is not only desirable but necessary in order to implement the demands of love and justice. One of the greatest problems of history is that the concepts of love and power are usually contrasted as polar opposites. Love is identified with a resignation of power and power with a denial of love.... What is needed is a realization that power without love is reckless and abusive and that love without power is sentimental and anemic. Power at its best is love implementing the demands of justice. Justice at its best is love correcting everything that stands against love. (King, 1967)

CHAPTER 6

The Moral Dimension of Human Resource Development

Introduction

This chapter attempts to map out a framework for understanding the moral dimension of human resource development in education. While acknowledging the usefulness of both the more traditional ethical analyses of educational administration (Strike, Haller, & Soltis, 1998; Maxcy, 2002; Nash, 2002), and more recent attempts to open up more synthetic and late modern perspectives (Starratt, 1991; Haynes, 1998; Furman, 2003; Shapiro & Stefkovich, 2001), this chapter attempts to name a deeper substratum of moral issues at the core of the educating process which call forth specific, proactive, moral responses from human resource leaders. Working with a more focused attention to the specific ethics of the professional practice of educating in a formal schooling context—that is, beyond the use of general ethical frameworks of justice, care, and critique—enables the development of a vocabulary and a series of analytic lenses for human resource developers to name their experiences as they face the moral challenges of leadership within the present context of their schools.

The Virtues of Human Resource Leadership in Education

In the field of ethics, one school of thought prefers to focus on ethical virtues rather than on ethical principles or ethical rules (Hursthouse, 1999; Walker & Ivanhoe, 2007). Virtue ethics focus more on the seeking of a moral good rather than avoiding a moral evil. Frequently, the virtue is the positive side of the negative activity prohibited by a rule: the virtue of honesty or truth-telling is the positive side of the negative activity of lying. This chapter will emphasize specific virtues of moral leadership within the profession of formal education, rather than the abstract principles intended to regulate ethical violations.

In the field of ethics, one finds a distinction between general ethics and applied, professional ethics. General ethics as it would be found in education deals more with the ethics of everyday life as that gets played out in the lives of most people in whatever context they find themselves. In the context of schools, general ethics involves issues around fairness, truth telling, respect, equity, negotiating conflict and misunderstandings, and correcting structural injustices embedded in the organizational arrangements of the school. Employing frameworks from the ethics of justice, care, and critique enables educators to name those general moral issues that face people in all walks of life and in all professions (Starratt, 1991). Applied or professional ethics has much more to do with the ethics of the profession *as a profession*. Part of professional ethics is about preventing harm in the practice of the profession. Often codes of professional ethics state what professionals should not do in their practice of their profession. Part of that ethics is about promoting the "good" essential to the practice of the profession. Medical ethics is concerned with promoting the good of its professional practice, which is physical health. Business ethics is supposed to be concerned with promoting the public and individual good involved in trade, commerce, and contracts. What is the good that the profession of education is supposed to pursue, promote, support? It is the good of learning. And what is the good of learning? It is the good of discovering, naming, constructing oneself as one is formally and systematically introduced to the natural, cultural, and social worlds that constitute one's public "situatedness," as well as learning the rights and responsibilities of being a member of those worlds. The good of learning implies coming to understand how and why to participate as citizens of those worlds. Moral educational leadership then means the proactive pursuit, cultivation, and support of those goods of learning in and for a humane community and polity. Those goods are intrinsic to the practice of formal education (Starratt, 2007).

Scholars have done a reasonably good job of describing the general ethics of educational leadership (e.g., Strike, Haller, & Soltis, 1998; Nash, 2002), but not a good enough job of describing what the proactive pursuit of those goods of learning might look like. Involved in that proactive pursuit one practices the virtues associated with the professional practice of educating. Those virtues of the practice of educating reflect leadership virtues. Here we focus on three that seem especially pertinent to the professional work of formal schooling: authenticity, presence, and responsibility (Starratt, 2004). We have already introduced the virtue of responsibility and the virtue of authenticity in much of what has preceded, but a brief recapitulation may serve to clarify our focus.

The Virtue of Authenticity

As we have seen in earlier chapters, authenticity is a necessary virtue for teachers to practice in their professional lives. Authenticity implies being true to oneself, owning oneself in one's professional practice, in one's working relationships. When others are in the presence of authentic people, they sense that these people speak themselves truly—that is, they are as they appear to be; there is little contrivance about them; they are relatively transparent and not afraid to be so. By and large, when they are with people, others are comfortable being authentic themselves.

The virtue of authenticity implies that being authentic is a good in itself; authentic people are more human than inauthentic people. Inauthentic people somehow have not reached a level of maturity in their humanness that authentic people have. Being authentic does not mean being perfect; rather, it means owning and accepting oneself with whatever talents and whatever limitations and imperfections one has. It also means being "up-front" in one's relationships, being present to the other person, being *there* in the now of the moment.

Being authentic in one's social and professional roles also implies a good in itself. Being an authentic father, an authentic neighbor usually implies being a good father, a good neighbor—again, not necessarily perfect, but one whose efforts, despite shortcomings, are sincere and well meaning. In one's profession or career, one can function authentically or inauthentically. One can be a careless auto mechanic or building inspector whose work lacks certain skills and understanding necessary to do reliable work. When these are joined to an attitude of not caring, of not taking pride in the work, then others will remark, "He's not a *real* mechanic." "She's a *bogus* building inspector." Likewise with the profession of teaching—some are recognized as authentic teachers, others as inauthentic. In teaching, being an authentic teacher involves the following competencies: a good understanding of the material being taught, a professional mastery of a variety of pedagogical strategies, as well as caring relationships with learners. Much the same holds for educational administrators: some have the capacities for administrative educational work which, when suffused with their personal authenticity, enables a veteran teacher to say, "Now that's what I call a *good* administrator; she knows what she's doing, she understands the complexities and demands of the classroom, she really listens to our stories, and doesn't promise what she can't deliver." Clearly, there are connections between authenticity in one's personal life and in one's professional life. However, authenticity in one's work requires levels of job-related competencies beyond those expected in private life.

One's sense of authenticity as a professional, however, is not a static, uniform thing. As we saw in chapter 2, one's sense of oneself changes as one moves through various life-cycle challenges, leaving one with new challenges to integrate earlier stages into more mature expressions of trust, autonomy, initiative, industry, identity, and so forth. As one grows as a teacher or administrator, one recognizes that the challenge of generativity in that professional role involves taking on new initiatives, acquiring new skills and understanding through various initiatives of trial and error on the job, industrious application in graduate programs and professional seminars, and developing one's professional identity within the challenges of accountability for responding to state mandates and policies.

Thus, one's own sense of being an authentic educator sometimes is called into question as one continues to respond to new challenges. One has to be able to look at oneself in the mirror every day and take stock of how much more there is to learn, how better to respond to the remains of yesterday's crisis, how to reach the person who always seems to disagree with the direction the school is moving in. As Richard Elmore suggests, a good human resource leader does not pronounce judgment on the work accomplished, but always asks, "What more remains to be attended to in this work?" (Elmore, 2008).

In this sense, one can never take one's authenticity for granted. It is always something to be validated in each day's adventures. Furthermore, one is not always happy with the day's performance of oneself; for the authentic person, that leads to greater self- knowledge and becomes tomorrow's challenge. For authentic educators, the challenge of authenticity is not so much about boosting one's self-esteem; rather it is about *attending authentically to the good* of the communal work of teaching and learning. The authentic educator lives with the daily challenge of effecting that good, despite institutional and personal limitations.

The authentic human resource developer, then, is a person who supports, stimulates, and activates the human resources that those in their charge bring to the work of learning. Through authentic involvement in promoting the good of their work, the human resource administrator practices the leadership virtue of authenticity. Reflecting back on the earlier chapters, we can now understand that the involvement in all the earlier dimensions of human resource development (human, organizational, professional, political) has a moral side to it. Through the practice of the virtue of authenticity, the human resource administrator enriches and deepens the work in the other dimensions of the work.

The Practice of the Virtue of Presence in Human Resource Leadership

The virtue of presence requires a somewhat lengthier treatment since it involves a vocabulary seldom used in the literature about education, or, indeed, in the literature about ethics. As we will see, it is both a psychological disposition as well as a virtue acquired through moral discipline.

Being fully present means being wide awake to what's in front of us. It could be another person, a passage in a book, a memorandum one is composing to the staff, a flower on one's desk. Being present is like inviting a person or an event to communicate or reveal something of itself. We cannot be present to the other if the other is not present to us; the other's presence must somehow say, this is who I am, this is what I am feeling about this situation, this is the part of me that I want you to really consider right now.

Being present means taking the other inside ourselves, looking at the other really closely, listening to the tone of the other, the body language of the other. This being present is also an unspoken message to the other that one is there, attending to the other's message, responding to the other from one's own spontaneous authenticity. Being present means coming down from the balcony where one was indifferently watching others' performance, and engaging them now with a full attention and risking the spontaneity of the moment to say something unrehearsed, something that *responds* to the authenticity of the other from your own authenticity.

This way of being present does not mean that one disregards the organizational context that colors every situation. Nor does it ignore the organizational roles one is called upon to act out. It does mean, nevertheless, that it is an exchange between human beings whose lives spill over beyond the boundaries of the organization and the organizational roles they play. The risk of spontaneous exchange does not assume that the exchange is free from all boundaries. Rather, the exchange tacitly acknowledges those organizational boundaries as well as societal cultural boundaries, but seeks within those constraints something genuine, something authentic between two human beings. What their meeting enacts, while subjected to the artifice of all social exchange, is a human work, something that provides some kind of support and satisfaction, along with dignity and honor.

People are present both as who they are and the roles they perform; they are present to the other in the ways they read the language, posture, gesture of the other as signaling what is going on inside. Professional people, whether architects, lawyers, doctors, sociologists, grammarians, literary critics, psychologists, biochemists, mathematicians, and airport security personnel, are trained to be present to the insides of things. They see the surface and discern the inner structures, processes, histories, aspirations and values. In fact, being present is a form of knowing (Polanyi, 1966). It is also a form of disclosing, of invitation, of communication and communion. Being present disposes one to act in response to the other, due to the knowledge communicated by mutual presence of one to the other.

We are present to something as who we are. If we are bigoted, we are present to something whose presence for us is already distorted by our bigotry. We are also present with our human history. Sometimes that presence involves ineradicable memories of sexual abuse in childhood, sometimes memories of a childhood in a loving family, sometimes memories of a lifetime of discrimination. How the other is present to us depends on our predisposition to be present to the other in a certain way, and our predisposition to allow the other to be present to us.

Does this being more fully present require something of us? It certainly does. It requires us to remove ourselves from occupying the center of the universe. It requires a certain self-displacement, letting others enter our space, monitoring our tendency to judge on first impressions, listening attentively to what the person is trying to or needs to say, and then actively engaging that person in authentic conversation. Such proactive presence flows out of some tacit awareness that this is the way humans are supposed to treat one another, that this way of relating to one another is something that sets humans apart from everything else in the universe. Our presence contributes to and enhances the human and natural energy in our surroundings.

There is a negative ethical obligation to presence and a positive proactive ethical obligation to presence. That is, we are under an implicit moral imperative to be present to the people and things around us. Being half-present may very easily be the cause of harm to another, whether we are driving a car, making a joke, making love, keeping accounts, or teaching. We have a negative obligation to avoid being half-present. There is also a proactive sense in which being present is expected of us if we are to be authentic and if we are to be responsible. Being present enables, indeed, encourages us to be authentic and to be responsible. Our presence activates our authenticity and the authenticity of others. That is why this kind of presence is a virtue: it produces good.

There are three ways of being present that suggest an ethical dynamic for educational leaders as human resource developers: an affirming presence, a critical presence, and an enabling presence.

Affirming Presence

Affirming presence involves foregrounding an attitude of unconditional regard for the person or persons you are working with. It means that you acknowledge them as they present themselves, not as you would like them to be, or not to be. It means not only holding them interiorly in high regard, but also explicitly telling them that in a variety of ways. More than anything, the message will be picked up quite clearly in the leader's actions. Those actions will communicate the following unequivocal messages: Each and every person enjoys an intrinsic dignity and worth; we expect people to reach out and help one another here; we believe that every person has an abundance of talents and good ideas and, given some encouragement, will enrich the life of the community.

The work of learning provides the underlying institutional context for an affirming presence. The school is a public institution serving the community with a mission of educating all children to the best of their ability. Thus, the affirming presence of the human resource leader is an affirmation in the context of the common commitment of the community to work together to promote a quality learning environment for all of the students. Within that mission, teachers, counselors, students, parents, nurses, social workers, custodians, secretaries, bus drivers, cafeteria workers, and others bring their human talents and skills to the work of that mission. The work of learning, however, is not engaged by robots, each performing in a pre-programmed function. Learners are human beings engaged in very risky work, the daily work of overcoming ignorance and confusion and obsolete understandings. It is risky work because, in the process, fragile human beings are potentially exposed to embarrassment, ridicule, and humiliation in the public forum of the classroom as they struggle to grasp what the teacher and the curriculum is asking of them. For teachers still mastering their craft, there is the risky business of looking like a bungler in front of the principal visiting their classroom. The institutional context of the work of learning, which itself carries intrinsically moral overtones (Starratt, 2003), requires an institutionally grounded ethical demand for an affirming presence. In order for the work of learning as a *human work* to flourish, it demands an affirming presence.

Within such an educating community, everyone is affirmed; the metaphor of family is invoked; celebrations of achievement are visible all around the school; photographs of teams of teachers and teams of students involved in a variety of projects adorn the school bulletin boards. When people in the school are in the presence of one another, even on bad days, there is clear evidence of respect, humor, sharing of ideas and criticisms, shouted greetings, plenty of "thank you," "good work!" and "we need to talk about that."

Almost always, the affirming presence of the human resource leader generates an affirming presence among the staff and students. However, the affirming leader will also attempt to build in structures and processes and rituals within the school week, month, or semester for the community to express affirmation for one another and for the continuing development of a strong sense of community. Sometimes that involves a more formally structured process for communicating with parents; sometimes a student forum for airing grievances and seeking reconciliation among conflicted groups within the school; sometimes a series of sharing sessions with the teachers' union officers; sometimes a faculty musical comedy depicting the foibles of the adults in the school. However those rituals are expressed, one thing will be constant: the affirming presence of leaders throughout the building, greeting others, encouraging, cheerleading, supporting, and consoling.

Enabling Presence

A second form of ethical presence flows from the affirming form of ethical presence. Through enabling presence one responds to the possibilities and the predicaments of the other, and explores the enabling aspects of situations and arrangements. An enabling presence starts with the premise: I can't do it alone; you can't do it alone; but together *we* can do it. An enabling presence signifies that one brings oneself fully into the situation with the other person. Again, the institutional setting of the school with all its limitations as well as potential, its constraints and its capacities contextualizes every situation.

Sometimes that enabling presence is predominantly a listening presence in which a teacher or parent needs to explain a problem or propose an idea that could be adopted by the school. In that case, an enabling presence communicates both a respect for the other, as well as a confidence that the other already may have the answer they are seeking, but needs to explore its dimensions more explicitly. An enabling presence also has to trust the good judgment of the other in the process of letting them try out something that is quite new to the school. The enabling leader also communicates a mutual taking of responsibility for the risks involved, and therefore the need to surround new ideas with the appropriate safeguards and institutional supports.

In other circumstances, an enabling presence might be more proactive, encouraging teachers to look at various examples of research-grounded best practices that might be adapted to their own teaching-learning environments. Some administrators' enabling presence leads to a more institutionalized practice of teacher-leadership committees, where teachers are supported in their efforts to establish project teams of peers who will explore new technologies of instruction, new assessment techniques, and the development of in-house rubrics for looking at student work. Taking it further, some administrators' enabling presence will encourage groups of students to develop their own initiatives around peer tutoring, new aspects of student government, or student-led ways to resolve conflicts among the student body.

This kind of enabling presence is concerned with capacity-building. In the national emphasis on school improvement and accountability, capacity-building appears at the top of administrators' agenda (Adams & Kirst, 1999, Elmore, 2008). Capacity-building, however, is not simply a bureaucratic matter of policy implementation. It is also a matter of deep conviction about the ways human beings ought to be present to one another, and about bringing that conviction into the institutional setting of the school—whether or not the state policy makers think it is a good idea.

The leader's enabling presence takes account of the institutional mission and the institutional constraints and possibilities of schools. An enabling presence, however, also brings an affirming presence, a spirit of openness to others, a welcoming of people as who they are: a mix of talents and interests, of hopes and fears, of strengths and fragilities. What is possible for the school, for teachers, and for students will be constrained by institutional policies and resources, to be sure; but those constraints can be transformed into possibilities, and those possibilities enlarged, by the creativity and talent of the teachers and students who feel affirmed.

The leader's enabling presence will have to attend to building specific capacities among the teachers, given the agenda of school reform. Those capacities include the developing of greater diagnostic sensitivity to how children learn and do not learn; a greater attentiveness to the so-called low achieving students in order to unlock their learning potential and to provide those institutional supports they need in order to improve; a more careful calibration of school rubrics for assessment; a more diversified approach to teaching reflective thinking and creativity; a more careful familiarity with diverse cultures in order to bring insights from those cultures into the classroom to enrich the learning of all.

On the other hand, the leader's enabling presence should also encourage a much greater development of the creativity of each teacher to enliven his or her classroom for learning. Even the so-called school improvement capacity-building lists can be carried out in the same deadening classroom pedagogies. To be sure, teachers are not in the entertainment business. But classrooms definitely need an enormous infusion of imagination, humor, and adventure to enliven the learning process. Rationality is a good thing, but humans are not simply logic machines. They need to perceive the underlying drama in life, the beauty and the pathos, the mystery and the complexity of the world in order to be attracted to studying the world. Teachers who bring an enabling presence into the classroom will explore with their students how to make the classroom learning come alive. They won't be satisfied with one new teaching strategy. They will keep coming back until the classrooms bubble over with excitement and enthusiasm. That enthusiasm will be fed by teachers and students exploring how to apply their learning to issues and concerns of the local community.

Leaders with an enabling presence will develop what is known as a spirit of efficacy among the teachers and students (Ashton & Webb, 1986). That spirit signifies that teachers, both individually and collectively, grow to believe that there is no student that they cannot reach in some significant way or other, that there is no pedagogical problem that they cannot find reasonable solutions to, when they collectively put their minds and imaginations to work. A spirit of efficacy is not a Pollyannaish claim of omnipotence; rather, it is a pragmatic understanding that every situation can be improved, not to perfection of course, but increasingly improved over time. Similarly, the enabling presence of administrators and teachers can lead students to develop an increasing attitude of efficacy, of "I can do this" or "we can do this." This is not to deny the reality of temporary failure. But the efficacious attitude toward learning expects to learn from failure and to make improvements the next time around.

By contrast, the administrator who is half-present to teachers and students comes to accept average performance as good enough, to be satisfied that the school is performing well if the teachers are at the front of the room and the students are in their seats, there are no fights in the cafeteria, and the football team wins some of their games. The half-present administrators fails to see how much time is being wasted every day, students' time being wasted by boring classes, teachers' time being wasted filling out forms and attending meetings where teaching and learning are trivialized into bits and pieces. The half-present administrator fails to see the enormous potential residing in every teacher and every student, a potential that is anesthetized every day by school routines that ensure a modicum of control and a minimum of commitment to the work of learning. The enabling administrator brings an enormous reservoir of hope and expectation to encounters with teachers and students, asking questions like, "Is that all you expect of the students?" "Is that all you expect from going to school?" "Is that all we expect of ourselves?" Those questions suggest that sometimes an enabling presence becomes a critical presence.

Critical Presence

Critical presence is a form of presence that calls attention to expectations regarding the work. Critical presence, therefore, need not be negative. Critical presence also calls attention to a good performance, very much like the theater critic will do in reviewing a good acting performance. Teachers and students need to know that their work meets and exceeds expected standards. Human resource leaders will be generous in their commendations of good work, letting teachers and students know that they are present to quality performances.

The opposite side of a good performance, however, is a mediocre or poor performance, and the human resource leader does not shrink from identifying what appear to be problematic parts to the performance. In being critically present in this way, however, the human resource leader will be sensitive to the person's human need for self-esteem, and encourage the teacher or student to reflectively evaluate those weak parts of the performance, more by asking questions than by pronouncing judgments.

Another aspect of critical presence involves interpersonal misunderstandings and conflicts. A critical presence in an encounter with the other can work in two directions—in a critical appraisal of oneself as the cause of a blockage to authentic communication because of some real or perceived harm to the other; or in a critical appraisal of something in the other's presence that blocks a mutual ability to communicate authentically. Critical presence attempts to name the problem that stands between the two parties. Naming of the problem, however, should not be one-sided. Both parties have to be present to the other, to listen to each other present its case, and then see what the situation asks of both.

Critical presence should not be a haphazard occurrence. It should be an enduring predisposition that acknowledges ahead of time the reality of messes that humans make—interpersonal, institutional, and policy messes. Critical presence is not based on cynicism, but rather on compassion and hope for the human condition. It is based on compassion for a humanity that aspires to high ideals, yet whose fragility and vulnerability lead to overestimating possibilities or to shrinking back in fear of the risks involved. It is based on hope, for humans have demonstrated time and again a resilience that transforms oppressive situations into a courageous response of the human spirit to create new possibilities. Finally, it is based on an enduring sense of responsibility to make the core work of the school—teaching and learning—work for the benefit of young people.

Another crucial aspect of critical presence involves a critique of structural arrangements in the school that privilege some and disadvantage others. Examples of such structural arrangements include a one-size-fits-all set of textbooks; a one-size fits-all daily class schedule, weekly schedule, semester schedule, and assessments; a one-size-fits-all opportunity to learn the material that will be tested. These arrangements guarantee a predictable percentage of academic "failures," those who are euphemistically labeled "underperforming," and a predictable percentage of successful students whose home education mostly accounts for their readiness to succeed in school (Coleman, 1966).

Human resource leaders, critically present to these structural arrangements, work to provide differentiated instruction, use a variety of curriculum materials, provide various time frames for learning, try to connect the learning tasks to life experiences of the learner, establish collaborative learning groups, create collaboration with parents and caregivers to support learning at home (Starratt, 2003). Critical presence to disadvantaging conditions at the school leads to a proactive taking of responsibility to counteract and to change those conditions.

The Virtue of Responsibility in Human Resource Leadership

We want to remind ourselves that we are speaking of the virtue of responsibility within the perspective of applied ethics, that is, the ethics that pertain to the profession of education. As such, the ethical virtue of responsibility relentlessly urges the professional to promote the moral good of learning: the development of the fullest humanity of the individual learner. The virtue of responsibility can be understood in both a negative sense and a positive sense. From the negative perspective, a human resource leader would be responsible to prevent or correct anything in the school that would impede the learning process. Often, educational administrators believe that they have fulfilled their moral responsibilities when they have provided for adequate safety and security measures in the school, when the students and teachers can go about their daily routines without fear of violence or other disruptions due to breakdowns in the functioning of the school facilities. Other administrators would add that their professional and moral responsibilities also include providing for an equal opportunity for all students to use the resources provided by the school (such as library facilities, computers, science labs).

Under stricter accountability policies in the United States, educators are now asked to assume even greater responsibility, namely, the responsibility to see that all students achieve passing grades on state administered tests. From this perspective, human resource administrators have specific responsibilities to hire and develop teachers who know the material in the curriculum in sufficient depth so as to understand the multiple applications of the curriculum standards towards which the state tests are targeted. Furthermore, these teachers are expected to scaffold learning activities to enable learners to translate the subject matter into terminology and examples that their younger, less mature minds and imaginations can comprehend. Thus, one can begin to discern that there is a moral responsibility of the human resource administrator, precisely as an educator, to hire competent teachers, and to monitor and cultivate the development of their practice of teaching (Sergiovanni & Starratt, 2006).

The moral responsibility of the human resource leader, however, goes farther than that. It involves a proactive moral responsibility to see that the learning achieved by learners in the school is itself authentic learning, namely "real" learning, not make-believe, superficial learning. Learning becomes real when it blossoms into an insightful connection to the intelligibility of a piece of the world—when the world speaks back to the learner, when the learner can say, "So *this* is what you are; so *this* is how you work; so *this* is why I should pay attention to you; so *this* is what you have to say to me." Involved in that insight is the insight, at least tacit into her or himself is being in *this* kind of intelligible relationship to *this* piece of the world. Educators captured by a sense of responsibility to nurture the good of learning will not stop trying to nudge the learner into insight until the learner looks up with a glow in her face and triumphantly announces, "I get it! I see what you've been trying to get me to see." This is the moral good which the responsible educator proactively promotes (Starratt, 1998, 2007).

The activity of attempting to learn should respect the integrity of what one is seeking to know. The learner should not approach the study of something superficially or carelessly, for that violates the intrinsic integrity of what is being studied. If the learner consciously misrepresents what he is supposed to have learned, then there is a violation not only of the integrity of what one is studying, but also the integrity of the learning process itself. This is most obvious in the case of an ideological reduction of facts to one dogmatic, or self-promoting interpretation—as may be found in politics, accounting, and warfare. The more subtle case involves the impersonal representation of someone else's right answers to test questions where one has no personal investment in the knowledge one is regurgitating.

Educators who fail to insist on the integrity of knowledge with their students can be accused of a kind of ethical laxity. Those who simply gear the work of teaching and learning to the achievement of high scores on tests, with little or no regard for the lasting meaning and significance of the subject matter, are teaching at best a superficial pursuit of knowledge and at worst a meretricious mistreatment of knowledge which empties the pursuit of knowledge of all but a crassly functional and self-serving purpose. That is to encourage a continuous violation of the integrity of learning and is, as such, a prostitution of the learning process. As that metaphor implies, the student is taught to feign learning to please those in authority—teachers, parents, politicians—in exchange for the coin of the realm in schools, namely, grades.

Human resource leaders also need to attend to this ethical enactment of responsibility. It is their responsibility to see that the teaching and learning going on in the classroom does not violate the content and process of learning, that learning and teaching is indeed of a high level of ethical enactment. That means a commitment through the hiring, evaluation and professional development procedures that (a) teachers will know well the curriculum they are expected to teach; (b) they will know how to communicate that curriculum in a variety of ways that enable youngsters to comprehend and appreciate many facets of what they are studying; (c) they will know their students well, and therefore can scaffold the learning tasks to respond to the background, interests, and prior experience of their students; and (d) they will insist that students take away from their learning important life lessons that will shape how they look upon the natural, cultural, and social worlds, and appreciate their own human adventure more deeply because of their studies. By cultivating these aspects of teaching and learning throughout the school, human resource leaders will be fully enacting the virtue of responsibility as educators.

Another perspective on the moral dimension of human resource leadership has to do, as was implied in chapter four, with their actual and potential influence on the organizational structures and processes of the school. The human resource leader, with a focus on improving the conditions of work for the primary human resources in the school—the learners—has access to the levers of organizational decisions concerning structures and processes that affect the core work of teaching and learning. These structures and processes are not ethically neutral. They either promote the integrity of the core work of the school—authentic learning—or they curtail or block the integrity of authentic learning. Often they do both at the same time. That is, they work to the advantage of some students, and to the disadvantage of other students.

Teacher evaluation schemes are another example of how many schools use a one-size-fits-all process to reward some teachers and to intimidate or frustrate others (Danielson & McGreal, 2000; Sergiovanni & Starratt, 2002). Some teacher evaluation schemes sustain intimidating power relationships that routinely issue negative or paternalistic judgments from superiors. Veteran teachers and administrators are resigned to the evaluation process as a burdensome bureaucratic task. One problem with many evaluation schemes is that they are such a colossal waste of time for everyone involved. Danielson and McGreal present, by contrast, a comprehensive teacher evaluation system that attempts to actually benefit both teachers and students. Their system is particularly sensitive to the ethical treatment of allegedly ineffective teachers by imposing obligations on the school system to show that it has done its part in providing generous remediation support to the teachers so classified.

The subtle bias in the various classifications of some children as special education children (Hehir, 2002), the tracking of students into dead end, low expectation programs (Oakes,1985), the scheduling of the "best" teachers in honors classes and the least experienced teachers into the lowest performing classes—the list of organizational arrangements that disadvantage students in schools can go on and on. These are human inventions, not arrangements of divine decree. They can be changed by educational administrators so that more and more students have a better chance in schools. Human resource administrators who refuse to risk changing the organizational structures and processes in schools might be accused of ethical laziness in the face of the evidence of how these arrangements discriminate against some or, indeed, most of the students.

Human resource leaders want to transform the school as an organization of rules and regulations and roles into a much more intentional self-governing community. In such a community, initiative and an interactive spontaneity will infuse bureaucratic procedures with human and professional values. Such idealism does not ignore the need for organizational supports and boundaries. This leadership is compassionate and expects messes, but uses the mess as a learning opportunity rather than a self-righteous occasion for punishment.

At this level, the human resource leader has to be much more proactive than reactive. The human resource leader now focuses less on what should be avoided or prohibited and more about the ideals that should be sought, more on actively creating enhanced opportunities for human fulfillment of teachers and students through the work they co-produce. This is a distinctive, value-added moral leadership. It is a dimension that is often ignored in scholarly treatments of human resource administration in education. This kind of moral human resource leadership enhances the resources of a community of teachers and learners who are transforming the mundane work of learning into something that engages the deeper meanings behind the drama of the human adventure, meanings that implicate them in that adventure.

Summary

This chapter has conducted an exploration of important moral virtues of human resource leaders. We can see how these virtues challenge the human maturity of leaders, and at the same time how those virtues invite a reciprocal response from those in their charge. The exercise of these virtues in the professional work of these leaders reveals the human significance, indeed the beauty of adult human interaction to which that work can aspire. The impact of these kinds of adult models on the young learners can be especially profound. The kind of community that can be formed by a culture of authenticity, presence, and responsibility can itself be a form of teaching that the young learners absorb and imitate in their own relationships. The constant, formative examples of leaders throughout the system enacting these virtues, when combined with their influence on the professional development of their colleagues, and linking those two dimensions to the visionary focus of the leadership team presents a powerful model of this different kind of leadership.

CHAPTER 7

Leaders of Leaders of Human Resource Development

Introduction

This book deals with foundational aspects of human resource leadership in education. In this chapter, we turn to the leaders of leaders of human resource development. Though not qualified as such merely by their appointment to the position, superintendents and district level administrators, and principals should see themselves as leaders of leaders of human resource developers. That responsibility implies several things about the nature and quality of the *district system* of human resource development. This chapter attempts to elaborate on some aspects of that system of human resource development, focusing first on the leadership of the superintendent or chief executive officer of the school district, whatever his or her title might be. This section will be followed by a focus on a the system of leaders of leaders working under the direction of the superintendent, and then followed by a treatment of the coherent system of support structures to support a thorough-going focus on human resource development throughout the district.

The District Superintendent as the Leader of Leaders of Human Resource Development

The process of transformation of the school district through a primary focus on the development of human resources within the school system begins with the appointment of a superintendent who believes in the view espoused by this book, that a school system is all about educating the human resources of the young people in its charge through the quality of the human resources of the educators and staff in the system. The superintendent, in turn, recognizes that her or his role requires a modeling of the same qualities expected in all the leaders of leaders of human resource development throughout the system. As superintendents assemble and develop the district leaders of leaders, their teamwork will reflect a deep respect for the humanity of each other, a trust and transparency in their working relationships, a collaborative spirit in which their diverse talents and capabilities are brought to bear on their collective efficacy to lead and manage the complex system of supports for the schools within the district. In turn, that leadership team will embrace their responsibilities to assemble and develop the principals who will be the leaders of the leaders in their individual schools. That work will require the district team modeling for the principals the same attention to the human resources of the principals that are expected of the principals in their work with the humans in their charge. The tone set by the superintendent, then, is crucial for the quality attention to the human resources throughout the district, with the special message to all the adults in the system that their mission is the development of the human resources of the young people in their charge.

Lest we minimize the challenge for superintendents, it must be acknowledged that this orientation toward human resource development will more than likely require a significant cultural change within the district office. The superintendent will have to go through a lengthy induction period with her or his assistants and deputies wherein they learn, probably with the help of a professional facilitator, the lessons of teamwork, of open communication, of transparency, of disagreeing with one another over plans and projections, of learning to listen carefully to one another, of withholding judgment until everyone has had a say, of asking for peer critiques of one's proposals, of sharing turf, of learning to shut up and listen for a change, and so forth. Unfortunately, many superintendents and district authorities do not inhabit such a culture, and it will take some getting used to, never mind convincing others in the district that this will be the way the whole district is supposed to function.

The superintendent's team will have to continually repeat the message that the work of all the adults in the system should contribute to the rich development of all the young people in the school system through the mediation of both the academic work and the community building that is meant to accompany, engage, and enrich that academic work. This primary focus of the work of the adult members throughout the school system should permeate all the important decisions to be made by them, and should be the measure by which they asses the significance and efficacy of their work.

This message will not ignore their accountability to improve the test scores on state exams, but that accountability will be seen as enveloped by their larger accountability to promote the full human development of the young learners in their charge—the belief being that the larger focus on the human development of the students will positively affect the performance on state exams, while at the same time enriching the very learning the state exams are intending to promote, within, of course, a flexible timeframe that better accommodates the readiness and capacities of the learners.

Establishing the priorities implied by that message, the superintendent will work with his district team and the principals to focus on a learning process to be promoted throughout the district that will integrate the personal and social growth of the learners with their engagement with a curriculum that sparks their understanding of and an active involvement with the worlds of nature, society, and culture. To that end, the superintendent and her or his team of district and school based leaders will explore a system-wide approach to a variety of professional development initiatives to promote the further professional development of teachers to enable them to develop pedagogical strategies that will thus engage the learners in such a learning process.

With this priority focus on promoting authentic learning opportunities to develop the human resources of learners, the superintendent will also work with the leaders of leaders of human resource development in the system to develop support structures and processes that need to be developed so as to promote and maintain a focus on human resource development of the young learners. That effort will involve an exploration of the coherence of the school system's vision of who they are and the journey they are on, with the system's goals, its policies and operational procedures, its programs, and organizational structures. This exploration will necessarily involve the leaders of leaders integrating their management functions with their promotion of the vision of human resource development so that the system's structures and operations consistently reflect the vision rather than obstruct or simply ignore the vision. That integration of leadership and management is expected of the superintendent as well, while at the same time using the position of the superintendency to repeatedly articulate the vision that will energize specific district-wide initiatives (ISLLC Standard I, Council of Chief State School Officers, 1996, 2008).

The Role of A District Director of Human Resource Administration

The superintendent will work with a district system of leaders of leaders. One of the first leaders of leaders the superintendent will recruit and appoint would be the district leader of the position of Human Resources Administration. This person would be a person who also espouses the beliefs and ideals about human resource development. The superintendent would rely on this person on the district leadership team to continually remind them to stay focused on this priority in the midst of the various political pressures that might distract from this priority; indeed, to use the focus on human resource development to illuminate potential responses to political pressures.

The Director of Human Resource Administration will be responsible for setting up those support structures that will enable the many details of human resource development of the adult staff to be organized and sustained. While this person is not usually associated with the management of the education of the young learners, within the leadership focus espoused in this book, this person would be involved in many of the discussions of the district leadership team, especially when those discussion would involve the professional development of the staff, since budget allocations for supporting professional development are often contained within the budget of the Human Resource Director.

Furthermore, the Director of Human Resource Administration would also be responsible for interfacing with principals throughout the system, as they dealt with issues concerning evaluation and tenure for younger teachers, procedures for recruitment and hiring of teachers and support staff, issues with the teachers union around contract renewal or specific conflicts and grievances involving the contractual rights and responsibilities of teachers.

As the above suggests, the Director of Human Resource Administration would have to work closely with the local head of the teachers union, both to establish procedures for handling grievances, planning for contract negotiations, planning for anticipated budget cuts, as well as interpreting the implementation of various state wide policy initiatives. In all of these discussions, the Director of Human Resource Administration would have to bring the district vision of human resource development into the conversation as a way of viewing specific management concerns.

Leaders of Leaders: School Principals

School principals are much closer to the work around which the whole system of human resource development hovers, i.e.. the daily work of academic learning engaged by the young learners in school classroom, libraries, science laboratories, and the learning of living and working in a community engaged by the young learners in the corridors, the cafeteria, the gymnasium, the playground, school assemblies, clubs, student government, community service activities, school dances, councilors' offices, detention hall, field activities, and other co-curriculars. Principals are the in-house leaders of leaders of human resource development. They have to work with the school staff to attend to both the academic and community learning.

Again, they will often relate their daily decisions and interactions with the staff to the vision statement to provide a value perspective to the significance of their work together. A good deal of their influence on student learning will come from their interactions with the teachers and support staff as they engage them in exploring how to make the learning environment more supportive, their relationships with students more efficacious, and their work on developing learning activities stimulating and relevant for those in their charge. They have to keep reminding all the teachers and support staff of the learning involved with community building, exploring specific ways to capitalize on conflict situations to develop communication skills, develop emotional restraint, resist stereotyping, and engage in mutual efforts to understand the others' sensitivities and points of view. They will encourage multiple efforts at co-operative learning both in academics and community problem solving.

Principals will also work with in-house leaders of leaders (assistant principals, cluster leaders, department chairs, project directors, coaches) to help them expand the human resource development orientation in their work with the groups in their charge. This work will be ongoing, providing these in-house leaders of leaders opportunities to discuss issues and problems they face in the work with their respective groups, helping them brainstorm ways to improve their leadership of these groups. Principals may get some help in coaching the in-house leaders of leaders from the school's counseling staff, due to their own professional understanding of issues and perspectives in youth development. Of course, central to the work of the in-house leaders of students (the teaching staff) is their own attention to the large agenda of the students' human development. Their work may be facilitated by holding panel presentations by students at a faculty meeting where students air issues and problems they are having with both the academic curriculum and the community building curriculum. Individual teachers should be encouraged to hold similar discussions with their students at least once a semester. At least once a semester, the principal should devote one faculty meeting to air out issues and problems the teachers are having with their efforts to develop good working relationships with their students, and their efforts to develop more authentic learning of the academic and community curricula. Through these and other processes, the principal will attempt to keep the vision of human development of the young learners at the forefront of the thinking of the school staff.

District Support Systems for Human Resource Development

Earlier we had seen the importance of the leadership of the person at the district level who directs the office of Human Resource Administration. At this point, we will review the kinds of support systems that person will put in place through working with school principals and various teacher committees. While these systems require a healthy dose of technical expertise, they should be functioning under the guidance and spirit of the school's vision statement on developing the human potential of the school community.

By technical expertise we mean those functions traditionally associated with personnel management in any organization. Again, these technical functions take place within institutions of formal education and therefore should serve the vision and mission of educating the young. These technical functions include the following: recruitment planning and implementation; hiring procedures; induction processes; mentoring; due process concerns; supervisory evaluations for beginning teachers, tenured teachers; termination of contract procedures; professional development; contract negotiation; conflict resolution.

Recruitment Planning

Choosing qualified and committed staff is one of the most important responsibilities of educational human resource leadership. The quality of the learning in any school depends enormously on the quality of the teachers whose knowledge of their curriculum material, their knowledge of and caring for their students, and the inventive ways they create encounters between learners and curriculum—all help to create a lively learning environment. Going the extra mile to recruit, evaluate, and hire the very best teachers will go a long way to ensuring a school's success. Filling slots on the teaching faculty late in the season with barely qualified or weakly committed personnel will require a subsequent commitment of considerable resources to bring them up to acceptable performance, that is, if they do not leave their jobs in a year or two. More than a few principals have been overheard muttering, "I never should have hired that person in the first place," or "I knew it was a mistake to keep them on after their first year. Now, I can't get rid of them."

The large turnover in teachers leaving the profession after two to five years is alarming. Not all of the departures can be blamed on careless hiring procedures, but many can. Because the hiring process is time consuming, and the commitment of resources and personnel to accommodating the needs of first year teachers so considerable, having significant yearly turnovers can be a constant drain on faculty and administrators at a given school.

Careful planning, therefore, is a must. It starts with keeping abreast of local demographic birthrate statistics that indicate the size—more or less—of future school populations. Those statistics will indicate whether the school population will be declining—suggesting a needed shrinkage of the teaching faculty, growing—suggesting a needed increase in the teaching faculty, or remaining the same—suggesting a stable teaching faculty. Furthermore, those demographics may suggest fluctuations in the ethnic, racial, economic, and cultural composition of the student body—pointing to the need for retaining or advancing the cultural and language diversity among the teaching faculty. Recruitment planning should encompass five-year demographic projections, which should be updated every year. That five-year projection should also include projected retirements on the teaching faculty.

Projections, of course, are approximations, educated guesses, but they can be further nuanced into a best-case, worse-case scenario to provide further refinements to the plans. Whenever possible, anticipated openings for teaching positions should be identified in advance. Profiles of teacher qualifications needed to fill those anticipated openings should be drawn up. The same should be done for openings in counseling, health and social service, coaching, and support staff. These personnel projections should be coordinated with school district budget projections, with projections of state support, and with projections of building, classrooms, and other resource needs.

School systems currently appear to be facing significant financial shortfalls that, in turn, require cutting of programs and staff as well as increased class sizes. Schools and school systems that actively plan for several personnel scenarios will be able to avoid the severe loss of morale among their staff when they can buffer these shortfalls by reasserting the values guiding all personal decisions, by exploring a more careful alignment of human resources, such as scenarios of shifting some staff to reduced workloads, replacing retirees by realigning programs that can function with one less teacher, realigning clusters of teachers, or the downsizing of some elective or lightly subscribed programs. Obviously, the importance of having a good working relationship with teacher union representatives who can be included in developing these fall-back plans cannot be overstated. All decisions involving reductions due to decreased funding are painful, but the pain is alleviated somewhat by anticipating those decisions and seeking the best solutions to the problems with the appropriate involvement of those likely to be affected by those cuts. Obviously, this kind of planning should reflect a deep regard for the humanity of people whose jobs and careers can be affected.

Recruiting

A recruiting process should be built into the yearly calendar of every human resource administrator. Sometime in the first semester of the school year, there should be a review of the projections for the following year derived from the five-year plan. These projections should be updated, surveying the potential and actual retirements, projected student enroll- ments, diversity and inclusion considerations, program needs, and budget projections. When possible, these projections should also include informa- tion about incoming children with exceptional needs that would require a teacher-aide. Job descriptions and position qualifications should be drawn up. One would hope that these job descriptions and qualifications would include the vision of human development espoused by the school, the core values of the school, and the expectation of authentic teaching consistent with the academic and community building curriculum goals. With these job descriptions in hand, the necessary clearances should be sought from the central office to begin recruiting for those anticipated positions.

In one sense, the annual recruiting process cannot begin early enough. Even before knowing the specific positions needing to be filled, human resource administrators should be in touch with their sources for staff candidates. By establishing good communications and trusting working relationships with these sources—nearby universities with strong prepara- tion programs, state professional associations who post job listings, state department of education web sites, other Internet-connected organizations who post job listings and job seekers—they will be better prepared to begin the recruiting season. Another source derives from informal communica- tions with other principals in the region who know of a qualified educator who will be available because of cuts in their system, whose spouse has taken a job requiring a move into your catchment area, or highly qualified applicants who did not make the final choice in their schools, and so forth. Again, these sources should be familiar with your demands for quality candidates, so that they will be the first filters that screen out mediocre candidates, knowing that they have little chance to be considered. Special care should be taken to seek sources for minority candidates in order to reap the benefits of diverse adult models, and diverse representatives of the various communities in the civic community.

Additional Internet sources are available that post job searches and job seekers for positions that, all things being equal, indicate a preference for qualified minority candidates, or candidates from under-represented com- munities. Because high-profile universities appear to majority-white school systems the most desirable sources for candidates, frequently minority candidates, educated at less well-known universities never make it to the applicant pool. Human resource administrators need to be proactive in making sure that their applicant pool includes minority candidates from many under-represented communities including English language learners and teachers who themselves have a disability. Moreover, they should seek an appropriate level of gender representation in the applicant pool.

Before initiating the annual recruiting process, human resource administrators should have prepared a document or statement that advertises the attractive qualities of the school. It is common practice now for every school to have a home page on the Internet, containing highlights of the school's strengths, visuals depicting the sense of community and élan at the school, a mission and core-values statement, and perhaps something about the high quality of the teaching faculty. Job searches should contain references to that home page, and to any other public documents that effectively market the school (media reports of various school accomplishments in the past three years, annual reports to the school committee, reports on outstanding students, teacher recognition and awards, and so forth). A rich portfolio of these documents should be updated annually and edited into a marketing-type document. Again, the document should reflect a sense of authenticity, not exaggerating the school's strengths, but presenting a truthful account of the many good things going on at the school.

The recruiting process should begin in the first half of the school year, or at least early in the second half of the year. That may occasion some personal recruiting trips to nearby universities, with personal conversations not only with department chairs, but also with program directors and individual professors who advise potential candidates for your anticipated openings. The ability to present your search using frameworks from the human resources professional dimension will clarify the kind of qualities you are looking for. The marketing materials, presented in an attractive brochure, can be left with these professors to make available to interested candidates. Direct interviews with potential candidates—obviously exploratory at this stage, may capture the early interest of highly qualified candidates, making your school the first to which they apply.

These targeted forays should be supplemented by postings on many available web sites that candidates are becoming increasingly likely to use early on in their search for potential positions. Those postings should include electronic links to the school's home page and other electronic information sources about the school. Attendance at job fairs or at local and regional educational conferences that provide recruiting stations, or at least for posting on job-listing bulletin boards, can also be helpful.

The job listing information should include directions on deadlines for submitting applications (preferably three months before the close of the current school year), as well as indicators of the type of information to be submitted about the candidates' qualifications. This information should include a resume, transcripts of degree programs and supplemental courses taken, letters of recommendation from university professors, former principals, field supervisors, cooperating teachers and administrators in schools where they completed their practicum projects, and a personal statement indicating why the candidate wants to work at this school, and what talents, values, and interests the candidate would bring to the job, including possible involvement in co-curricular activities.

As applications are received, they should be checked for completeness, and a letter sent out acknowledging receipt of the application, including an anticipated date when a successful candidate will be chosen. Some administrators prefer using this initial check for making a first judgment on the candidate's qualifications, placing those clearly unsuitable into one file, and the qualified candidates into another file.

Hiring

Without short-circuiting the hiring process, the school should seek to hire the top candidates for the available jobs well before the close of the school year. That would allow the incoming member of the staff to meet those veterans on the staff with whom the new person will be working, and to get a sense of what to expect in the coming year.
It will also help to avoid the problem of having to fill a position close to the opening of the next school year with candidates who have been already passed over by many other schools.

After the deadline for receiving applications, or even well before it, a hiring committee should draw up a list of desired qualifications to be met by the candidates. Frequently, a scoring schema is applied—say, a list of ten qualifications with a range of potential scores of zero to ten for each qualification. In some schemes, some qualifications might allow for higher scores than others because of their importance for the job. A list of possible qualifications might look something like the following:

- Quality of subject matter/academic background
- Teaching experience (including quality internship experiences in their degree program)
- Versatility and adaptability (potential to teach two academic areas; experience at more than one grade level)
- Diversity qualifications (including facility with a useful second language)
- Special needs qualifications
- Student welfare focus

- Quality of university/graduate programs attended
- Long-term career focus/commitment to the profession
- Maturity and other personal attributes
- Co-curricular qualifications
- Other considerations

Some would add the eleventh qualification in order to account for some unusual talent or capability that should be noted in the candidate's favor, in case there was a need to distinguish between two top candidates whose scores were just about identical. Using schema like the above is advisable not only for internal consistency in hiring practices, but also for legal reasons. Should one candidate claim some kind of unfairness in the hiring process, the school can document their attempt to be objective in matching the candidate's qualifications to the demands of the job.

After sorting through the applications and scoring each one, the committee should identify the top five prospects. They should then settle on the top three candidates, leaving the other two as back-ups, should it be impossible to hire any of the top three.

The hiring committee should be made up of two or more teachers, the human resource administrator, the principal, a parent, and, when the middle or secondary grades are involved, a student. The committee should then set up a schedule of interviews. Prior to the actual interviews, the interview committee should settle on an interview protocol. Again, it would be helpful to work out a list of questions each committee member will ask all the candidates, with a scoring system of points awarded for answers to the questions. Among those questions should be two or three cases of situations that tend to occur during the school year, requesting the candidate to describe how and why he or she would respond. In order to assure levels of consistency, they should work out rubrics for assigning higher or lower scores to answers to the questions. For example, the first question the committee might ask is, "Why do you want to work here and what do you bring to us that would want to make us hire you?" The committee would discuss a variety of possible responses, and then decide what kind of responses would earn a score of ten, what kind a score of five, and what kind a score of one or zero. This discussion and agreement about scoring various answers would go on for each of the questions they would ask. They might even want to print out a scoring sheet with each of the questions listed. They would question the candidates on topics such as the following:

- The candidate's philosophy of education; core values, educational platform

- A familiarity with the requisite curriculum standards for areas they would teach
- Possession of a portfolio of lesson plans from their internship in teaching
- Familiarity with working out rubrics for assessing student work, backward planning for curriculum units, data-grounded student assessment and remediation
- Their expectations of working conditions at the school; expectations of school district support
- Can they give examples of how they have worked with students of differing levels of readiness
- What are hopes for their own learning in their first year on the job?
- What are their greatest fears about their first year on the job?
- Familiarity with and examples of state requirements for accommodating special needs learners and English language learners
- If you were teaching (quadratic equations, cell division, gravity, poetry, Thoreau's *Walden*, etc.), what would I see your students doing?
- Ability to work with underperforming learners to bring them up to class levels of achievement; familiarity with differentiated instruction
- Give three examples of how you would enact core values in the classroom
- What interests you most in your academic specialization? What life lessons do you want your students to get from that academic area?
- Attitudes about and plans for working with parents
- How to deal with parents of an unruly student
- Attitudes about and abilities as a team player; collaboration with other teachers
- What would you do if … hypothetical cases of expected situations in the classroom
- Let's say the principal visited your class and found fault with your teaching. How would you like to get suggestions for improvement?
- What did you like most about your own K–12 schooling? What was disliked most about K–12 schooling? What was liked most about college experience? What was least?

The interviewing committee should feel free to ask for elaborations to responses to these topics and questions, as well as to request examples of what the candidate meant.

While the candidate has a bit of time to compose him or herself after the interview, perhaps to enjoy some refreshment in the teachers' room, the committee should complete their scoring of the candidate's performance and hand them in to the chair of the committee.

The principal then tallies the scores for the applicant's qualifications and for the interview. It may turn out that one candidate clearly stands out above the other two, in which case, the committee's job is fairly complete. If two of the candidates, however, have very close composite scores, then the committee will have to make a detailed analysis of the profiles of the candidates according to what their evidence indicates, and rate those profiles against the job expectations for that position. Sometimes it will come down to judging between two sets of desirable abilities and talents, and making a case for why it would be better to choose one person over the other. In any case, the principal should make sure to preserve the record of their discussions, as well as the scoring sheets for at least a year, to be available in case of a legal dispute over the hiring procedures. Hiring procedures and judgments are far from an exact science, but school officials should be able to provide evidence that they acted in good faith, basing their decisions on what they considered to be convincing evidence.

Shortly after the final decision has been made, and the successful candidate has signed a contract with the school system, letters should go out to all the applicants thanking them for their interest, and informing them that someone has been chosen for the job. More than a few candidates have had the exasperating experience of never hearing back from a school after it has gone through the hiring process. That is a violation of professional courtesy. In other cases, some principals will send a special letter of thanks to the final two candidates not chosen, acknowledging the school's appreciation of their talents and commitment, along with best wishes in their careers.

Induction

With the expected attrition in the teaching ranks due to retirements, shortages in available candidates are projected and, indeed, being reported. This phenomenon, added to the documented loss of over a third of new teachers in their first three years on the job, has led to a greater concentration on retaining qualified beginning teachers through a much more supportive induction process in the first three years of new teachers' experience at a school. These induction plans have detailed a number of user-friendly procedures and structures. Beginning with a one- or two-day retreat during which new teachers meet the principal and some of the veteran members of the staff to review what life at the school is like (with a stress on the positives), what are the core values and mission of the school and how they get embedded in daily procedures; what are the security policies in case of emergencies; what problems are likely to crop up and how to deal with them; what budgetary resources are available and how to secure some; whom to go to when certain situations arise; what the first semester schedule and calendar looks like, including sessions with parents.

Rather than have this initial experience be a top down series of monologues, there should be opportunities for new teachers to tell their stories and share their concerns and questions, to check out their classrooms and locate the supply closets and teachers' lounge, to meet the custodians, and exhibit some things they'd like to try with their students. Sharing in a picnic or cook-out in the park provides a pleasant ice-breaker. The purpose of these initial days is to build a sense of teamwork and community. Assuming that these new teachers will be assigned to mentors, the mentors should have an hour or more with their individual mentees to prepare for some of the initial sessions they will have together.

The induction process should continue throughout the first two, possibly three years. Working mostly in support groups, they should continue to explore curriculum content targeted toward required standards, varieties of differentiated instruction, varieties of assessments, backward mapping to lesson plans, diagnosing strengths and weaknesses in students' work, and so forth.

Mentoring

Each new teacher should be assigned a mentor who will work with them for at least a semester, if not for the first year or two of their induction period. Mentors should be chosen from the most talented teachers on the staff who can be good role models for beginning teachers. The mentors should undergo some preparatory planning sessions with either the principal or an experienced trainer or both, in order to be clear about their responsibilities. All mentoring activities should focus on assisting the beginning teachers to continue to improve their abilities to facilitate the learning for all the students in their classrooms. Of course, the mentor can also assist the new teachers in dealing with the unexpected—a particularly unruly student, a very demanding parent, an auto accident on the way to work. They can also counsel them about observing some of the unspoken rules among the faculty—rules about the faculty parking spaces, about arrival and departure times, about asking the custodians for help with a project, about not hoarding all the supplies, etc. The work of the mentors should be clearly delineated from the work of the principal with new teachers. Issues around confidentiality should be clarified ahead of time. For example, should the records from classroom visits of the mentor be part of the administrative decision regarding retention after the first year of teaching? New teachers should be encouraged to establish working relationships with other members of the faculty as well. The principal and one other teacher (not the mentor) should monitor the lesson planning, the assessments, variety of classroom teaching, response to special needs children, and so forth. Some of these supervisory sessions might very well turn out to be more helpful than the relationship with the mentor. Mentors, however, should receive a stipend for the extra time they devote to their mentoring responsibilities.

Due Process Concerns

Whether communicating with new teachers, with veteran teachers, with parents, or with students, it is important to be transparent about agreements, policies, and procedures. In other words, everyone should know—to the extent possible—what is expected of them, including the expectations of administrative responsibilities. No student should be suspended without prior knowledge that suspension was a sanction connected with certain violations of the schools rules. Furthermore, no student should be suspended without a chance to tell his or her side of the story. In other words, students, teachers, and parents have the right to present evidence that bolsters their side of the story, and to review the evidence of those lodging a complaint against them. There should be in place a written description of agreed-upon procedures to be followed when some kind of disciplinary action is contemplated against any member of the school community, including procedures and timetables for levels of appeal, clear statements of predictable sanctions for varying types of rule violations, arbitration procedures that may or may not apply to various situations. There will seldom be a perfect handbook of due process procedures because unforeseen situations and circumstances will inevitably arise. That said, those procedures should be periodically reviewed and updated to provide the greatest transparency of expectations for all. Such attention will often forestall lawsuits which otherwise could be both costly and trust-destroyers.

Teacher Evaluation

Connected to the issue of transparency, teacher evaluation policies and procedures should be well documented and periodically reviewed by the whole faculty with descriptions of the kind of evidence evaluators will seek in making their evaluations of teachers. Often teachers are faced with a checklist of things the supervisors will be using as evidence for rating a teacher, some of which might be quite superficial, while others which might be absolutely essential for making judgments about the teacher's ability to promote the learning of all the students (Danielson & McGreal, 2000; Scriven, 1990; Stodolsky, 1984). Many evaluation forms, however, do not seem to distinguish between the superficial and the important. Seldom do the items have differentiated scores attached to them. Furthermore, the checklist seems to imply that that all the items on the template can be applied to any and all teachers in any or all classrooms. This has led to the comical situation where—after the principal has sat through forty minutes of observing art students working on their painting or pottery in relative silence, with the teacher circulating around the room offering brief comments, pointing out some salient point to a busily engaged student— a principal will say to an art teacher "I'll need to come back when I can observe you teaching."

As was implied in the section dealing with the induction of new teachers, supervisors need to be clear with teachers in advance of any actual supervisory episode about the purpose and the process to be followed in that upcoming activity, as well as about the specific aspects of the classroom activity the supervisor will be evaluating. Normally, the supervisor and teacher will be able to refer to written documents that cover the major elements of a supervisory episode and refer to exemplary teaching practices. That will enable them, in early conversations about the upcoming classroom observations, to adapt the observational format to an agreed-upon focus.

A major shift in the focus of supervision activity has been occurring in the past decade or so—from a concentration on specific teaching behaviors (seemingly recommended by research on "effective" classroom pedagogy) to a concentration on actual student learning, successful or otherwise. Influenced by national policies that insist on schools' greater attention to improving the learning of underperforming students, supervisors have been working with teachers to diagnose the problems underperforming students are having with traditional classroom instruction and to devise a variety of differentiated pedagogical approaches that respond to these diagnoses. This attention to student actual learning has received further specification due to the insistence on curriculum and assessment standards that define the content of the curriculum that is to be learned. Thus, the work of supervisors with teachers has taken on a level of depth and complexity that had been lacking in much of prior supervisory practice.

To be more specific, and to repeat in summary fashion what has been outlined in previous chapters, supervisors have to attend to multiple factors in their conversations with teachers.

1. How well does the teacher know each student in the classroom— their family background, their prior academic record, their talents

and interests as well as their academic weaknesses, in order to bring them into a realistic dialogue with the curriculum material at hand?

2. Has the teacher developed a good working relationship with each student, such that the student feels respected and cared for by the teacher—a perception that serves as a motivational basis for investing the effort to concentrate on the learning tasks?

3. How well does the teacher know the subject matter of the curriculum, such that the teacher understands the significance of the curriculum standards to be met and can communicate that significance to the learners?

4. How well can the teacher adapt the teacher's understanding of the curriculum content in a variety of ways that differentially address the levels of readiness of the learners and connect the learning task to the past and present experience of the learners?

5. How clearly has the teacher developed assessment rubrics so that the learners understand what is expected of them beforehand, and so that the teacher can provide helpful feedback after the assessment exercise?

Needless to say, supervisors have to develop a greater understanding of and sensitivity to the complexities involved in the above topics of conversation, so that the conversations can flow from a more deeply shared set of understandings and commitments between the participants in the supervisory episode.

Another shift has been occurring in supervisory practice—the shift from an exclusive concentration on working with individual teachers one at a time, to engaging several teachers in a group setting in a focus on student work. These group conversations enable teachers to share ideas and insights and new pedagogical approaches to underperforming students and to the integration of standards into their assessments, and rubrics for assessments. Whether or not this work also includes actual classroom observations by the supervisor, or whether the supervisor's reports of the teachers' participation in these group sessions satisfies the evaluation requirement varies within and among school systems. In any event, such group work is becoming an alternative to the exclusive concentration on one-teacher-at-a time supervisory episodes.

The above example of an alternative to traditional supervision methods is but one of a growing number of alternatives within the large umbrella of supervisory practice. Some school systems allow for a two- or three-year hiatus between formal evaluations of veteran teachers with high competency ratings, providing the teachers are working on an approved professional growth plan. A variety of professional growth plans can satisfy this requirement: taking university courses in academic content areas to deepen their grasp of the material they are teaching; visiting classrooms in other schools or school districts; attending a series of workshops and seminars conducted by regional professional associations such as the Association for Supervision and Curriculum Development; or provided by a regional consortium of chapters of the teacher union. Other options include individual or group action research projects that focus on an important aspect of curriculum design or student assessment. In all of these cases, the supervisory system works closely with the professional development supports of the district to bring a greater synergy to bear on improving student learning for all.

One of the most difficult tasks facing a principal is the process of placing a teacher on probationary status and the accompanying possibility of terminating that person's contract. Again, the procedures involved should be spelled out so that the person involved understands each step in the process. At a minimum, those steps should include the following.

1. A clear statement that the teacher's classroom performance is unsatisfactory or in violation of the contract and of the professional behavior expected of a teacher. The statement should refer to instances where this unacceptable behavior was pointed out to this teacher, citing clear evidence of the unacceptable behavior, with warnings that, should the behavior continue, it would constitute grounds for suspending or placing the teacher into a probationary status.

2. In the case of clearly unprofessional behavior such as racial slurs in the classroom, multiple unexplained absences, failure to perform assigned duties such as monitoring school bus arrivals or departures, etc., the person may be warned that *any* continuation of those behaviors would result in the possibility of administrative termination of employment.

3. In the case of poor performance of teaching responsibilities, the teacher should be notified in writing of what the deficiencies are, and what steps the teacher should take to improve in those deficient areas. To show its good will intentions, the school system should offer various forms of support while the teacher works on improving elements in the improvement plan. The teacher should be given a reasonable deadline by which improvements should be in place, noting that at least three people will be involved in evaluating the teacher's progress, and noting the kind of evidence the school will require as evidence of improvement.

4. If the teacher's evaluations are positive, the teacher will be returned to the ranks of those teachers considered satisfactory, with the normal evaluation procedures to become operative again.

5. If the teacher's evaluations are negative (citing evidence to substanti-
    ate the negative evaluation), then the teacher will be put on admin-
    istrative probation, with the teacher's rights and responsibilities
    spelled out in a legal document that points to termination of the con-
    tract if the teacher fails to improve by a specified deadline. Again, the
    teacher should have access to some school resources that may enable
    the teacher to sufficiently improve, indicating good will on the part
    of the school system. Only after these good-will attempts have been
    exhausted should the underperforming teacher be notified of the ter-
    mination of his or her contract.

By and large the practice of teacher evaluation and supervision has
grown increasingly sophisticated, with clearer guidelines for the evaluation of pre-tenure teachers, differentiated from that of tenured teachers,
differentiated from that of the administrative evaluation of underperforming, unprofessional, or probationary tenured teachers. Human resource
administrators, principals, and department chairs will need to attend to
the coordination of the larger system of teacher evaluation, seeing that it
remains transparent, continuously updated in the light of the many initiatives within the school renewal agenda, urging the focus on continuous
improvements in student learning, and promoting emerging leadership
among teachers working on that agenda.

Professional Development

What has been said about teacher evaluation pertains to professional
development. Attention to the five questions asked above concerning
supervision should provide the overall focus of professional development
activities. Among policy makers and researchers, professional development has been singled out as the crucial ingredient in school improvement. However, the meaning of professional development has changed
significantly over the years, moving away from "drive-by" in-service days
that marked the disjointed practice of the past to a continuing, persistent,
and coordinated effort at improving quality learning for all students. This
change has placed the continuous work of the in-house staff to diagnose
student learning difficulties and to respond with more targeted and differentiated instructional interventions with diverse learners as the cen-
terpiece of professional development. Supports from outside coaches
and consultants are now focused on assisting in this core work. Human
resource administrators, other district administrators, and principals
need to coordinate the systemic initiatives and plans around this core
work, proactively securing budgetary and time and curriculum resources
needed for the work.

Conflict Resolution

In an ideal school, conflict might never occur. In the real world of all organizations, however, conflict is almost ever-present in some form or other. Besides having its source in misunderstandings, mistakes, bad luck, unforeseen consequences of a seemingly benign decision, conflict arises out of the heavy ego investment people make in their work, and in their need for a modicum of self-esteem. When another party seems to interfere with their area of responsibility, or someone claims ownership of what is considered their turf, or someone appears to belittle their contribution, or to appropriate some of their resources, or to attack their human dignity—then we observe the quick flare-up, the retaliatory accusations, the aggressive resistance. Furthermore, humans are not angels. They often make a mess out of things, sometimes intentionally, sometimes unintentionally. The result is a conflict that needs to be resolved before lawyers or the police are called in.

While the resolution of conflict is a responsibility throughout the school, those responsible for the system of human resource administration are often responsible for composing and administering the policies and processes of conflict resolution, especially when the conflict involves groups of persons or has progressed beyond individual attempts to resolve the conflict into a sequence of institutional appeals.

What has been said above about due process applies here. Attempts to resolve a conflict should include: a) an attitude of trust and respect towards all parties seeking redress; b) an opportunity for all sides to tell their side of the story; c) an effort to avoid *ad hominem,* personal attributions of illwill in the interests of articulating the substance of the conflict, beyond the clash of personalities; d) the marshalling of evidence to support one or more parties in the conflict; e) reference to existing, documented policies and agreements that might be called into play to settle the conflict; f) when appropriate, an effort to avoid a win-lose settlement in favor of a win-win resolution. In many conflicts, both sides have a legitimate point to make. Recognizing that reality, those arbitrating such conflicts should try to negotiate a settlement where not only the dignity of all parties is preserved, but also where all parties can walk away with a partial, however small, victory. Finally, in the course of the conflict resolution, there should be an effort at healing the emotional rift that may have occurred, encouraging each side to shake hands and to turn their attention to the larger goals that need their energies and talents. One of the lessons that may emerge in situations of conflict is that the conflict indicates a point of friction in the organization, where policies are ambiguous, where departmental boundaries and responsibilities overlap, where two administrative responsibilities contradict one another, or some other structural or procedural aspect of the organization is dysfunctional. The conflict points out these points of friction and suggests the need for improved alignment, or clarification of ambiguities in policies, structures or procedures. Thus, conflict is often necessary for improved organizational synergy.

Conflict can also be viewed as a healthy phenomenon. Often conflict arises from a disagreement over goals. The resolution of such conflicts leads to goal clarifications and possible realignment of commitments of the parties to the conflict. Conflicts sometimes arise out of attempted innovations, pointing to some unanticipated consequences of the innovation. Again, conflict helps to correct a problem. This attitude toward conflict can help those called upon to resolve it to see the positive potential outcome, instead of being drawn into the anxiety-inducing experience of finding the anger of the conflicting parties addressed towards oneself. It also emphasizes the importance of the healing role of the human resource leader, calling the attention of the parties that their disagreements have actually led to some beneficial adjustments to the future operations of the school.

Contract Negotiations

Contract negotiations between teacher unions or associations and the school board are among the most difficult and potentially demoralizing experiences for the whole school community. In the operation of any organization, resources are always limited and goals are always beyond the resources to achieve them in their entirety. This will always lead to the bargaining over which parts of the organization will get the favored share of the resources. One has to take the limitation of resources as a given, and hence the necessity of bargaining as a given. What needs to be avoided is the demonizing of the opposition for their ill will towards the other party, the attribution of selfish motives to the other parties, the laying down of ultimatums, and the shouting and finger pointing of unchecked emotions. One has to communicate a belief in the good intentions of the other party. On the other hand, one has to expect that the other party will start out with a position that represents a *start* in the bargaining process, with one or more fallback positions as each side indicates a willingness to give a little. If at all possible, the bargaining should involve the parties in direct, face-to-face communication, without the intermediaries of lawyers. Lawyers can work in the background with their respective clients, but should not engage in the actual face-to-face bargaining sessions. This is necessary to preserve the mutual assurances of good will of both parties.

Only when the bargaining breaks down with little hope of resolution should the process be referred to mediation. Both sides, however, should recognize beforehand the serious costs of becoming deadlocked, namely, the loss of morale among the teachers and staff, and the destruction of any semblance of good will on either side. School systems take years to recover from the anger, frustration, and cynicism engendered by bargaining stalemates. Even worse, the loss of enthusiasm and energy for continuing the school improvement agenda translates into the evanescence of political capital and financial efficiency as well.

Human resource leaders as we have conceived them in this book may have little direct involvement in the collective bargaining process. Nonetheless, they can have an indirect influence on it through their positive influence on faculty and staff attitudes and commitments within the schools. They can also have an influence through communications upward through the system that reveal the aspirations and attitudes of the teaching force as the time for collective bargaining comes about. After the collective bargaining is completed, they will also have to deal with the positive and negative feelings among the staff, providing some opportunities for expressing these feelings and clarifying, where possible, what resource options of the school board actually came into play. Nevertheless, the continuation of all the positive supports that human resource leaders have at their command will help the faculty and staff to refocus on the significance of the work in front of them, namely, improving the life chances of their students through the quality of learning experiences they create for them.

Conclusion

While this chapter has outlined many of the technical functions human resource leaders perform, we should remember that these functions should be suffused with the concerns developed in earlier chapters, namely concerns for the humanity and the human development of the faculty and staff and students; concerns for the ongoing professional development of the teachers; concerns to empower the teachers so that their unique talents can contribute to the communal efficacy of the faculty to respond to every student in their agenda of self-development; concerns that the very structures and procedures by which the school shapes and channels the learning of the students may privilege all, instead of only some students with high quality learning experiences. Technical proficiency in the traditional tasks of human resource administration devoid of these concerns can only carry a school so far. Integrating these concerns with technical efficiency can carry a school to heights of greatness.

CHAPTER 8

The Organic Interpenetration of Human Development Throughout the Work of Schools

A Different Leadership Challenge

In the past quarter century or so, the voices of the corporate world have influenced the rhetoric and the policy frameworks defining the schooling agenda. Not only in the United States, but increasingly so among both industrialized and developing nations, the language of investment, efficiency, productivity, and capital accumulation has crept into the ways governments think about schooling. The term "capital" has become a metaphor for the creation of resources and reserves—not simply in monetary terms—by, through, and with which countries, communities, and organizations develop a technological and cultural infrastructure that will increase their productivity. Just as countries and communities and organizations invest their monetary resources to increase productive capacities, so they likewise invest in human and social capital for meeting their long-range needs.

From this economic perspective, human capital means a labor pool that is well educated, highly skilled, inventive, and disciplined. Governments, communities, and organizations make investments in educational institutions and research centers for their long-term stability and growth within the world community. Likewise, governments, communities, and civic institutions have made investments in schools and universities to increase social capital.

Social capital means the creation of those reserves of social habits of cooperation, shared social goals, and shared social mechanisms whereby schools, universities, and research and development centers can appeal to common values, purposes, and futures which they and their surrounding communities share and embrace. Cooperation, collaboration, and social responsibility produce benefits for the civic communities that supply the students and staff and financial resources, benefits in the form of socially responsible, knowledgeable, skilled, and inventive citizens and workers who will sustain the economic and political viability of these communities.

Educating institutions, however, not only require mechanisms to create bridges to the families and communities that support them in order to enhance the social capital they share with these families and communities, they also need to develop internal human and social capital within their own walls. That is to say, they need to promote the growth of teachers in their own humanity and in their professional talents. Likewise, they need to build *internal* social capital of cooperation, participation and shared values among the students, faculty and staff. The faculty and staff will be far more productive in their work with young learners in an environment of human respect, support, collegiality, and shared commitments than in a depersonalized, hierarchical environment.

The orientation of this book embraces the goal of enhancing the internal human and social capital of the school as a good in itself, aware that a side benefit of this primary goal will be the gradual increase in the knowledge capital within the larger community. Significant investment in creating, accumulating and sustaining large reserves of human and social capital through a generous system of human resource development, it is argued, pays significant dividends in the human, intellectual, and moral development of young people in schools. The reserves of these kinds of capital will energize the efforts of faculty, staff, and students to improve the quality of learning—the primary work of schools. As is argued from the opening chapter of this book, the learning of the academic curriculum must feed into the students' agenda of self-construction, a task made clearer through the modeling of teachers who have themselves effected such an integration. The agenda of self-construction should not be seen as a self-centered, isolating agenda. Rather, the active development of autonomous individuals contributes to the overall health of communities and societies. An integrated balance between community building and authentic academic learning has been stressed throughout our argument.

Such an integration is more likely to occur in schools that invest heavily in creating reserves of human and social capital that energize the whole culture of the school. The return on this investment in human and social capital, it is argued, will be found in the growth of healthier human beings who discover their human fulfillment by a responsible participation in the social, cultural, and natural worlds they already inhabit, and who thus contribute to the human and social capital of their communities as good neighbors, active citizens, and productive workers.

The Mutual Interdependence of the Six Dimensions

It is important to recognize that each of six dimensions of human resource leadership implies the other five dimensions in a kind of hologram synergy. Each dimension requires the force and energy of the other five in its own completion. Thus, the first and most basic dimension of human resource leadership—acting humanely towards others—is assumed in the second dimension, promoting the professional growth of the faculty. Teachers bring the understandings of their profession—of human development, of learning theory, of responsive and variable pedagogy, of the content of the curriculum, of a variety of assessment protocols—to the service of young human beings. Their professional practice is adapted to the human variables they find in the diverse young people in their classrooms immersed in the throbbing buzz of their human existence. The personal curriculum of these young people is to learn the lessons involved in constructing their personal and social selves and their futures. Their personal curriculum needs to be connected to the academic curriculum of the school if the school learning experiences are to take on personal significance for these young learners. Teachers can do this by referring to how their own lives have been shaped by their education, providing examples of how the knowledge and values within the academic curriculum bring out the intelligibility of their own relationships to the natural, social, and cultural worlds.

The work of human resource development in promoting the continuous professional development of teachers takes place in the organizational setting of a school. Attention to the organizational dimension requires human resource leaders to deal with the tensions flowing from the fundamental paradox of organizational life, namely that it can be at one and the same time a painful limitation of human freedom and creativity even while it provides a resource-rich environment for the exercise of human freedom and creativity.

Organizations, though resource-rich, are also limited in the resources they can command. Schedules, calendars, the spaces available in the building—these and other organizational arrangements constrain a teacher and a student from, for example, prolonging a class just when it is heating up with student debate and focusing on key questions, or from going to the library to complete the chapter in that fascinating book when the schedule calls for the student to be in class. Teachers may want to take their classes on field trips, but the budget for class trips may already be exhausted. Football coaches and studio art teachers want more time for practice. The challenge for human resource leaders is to identify those organizational structures that most inhibit quality learning for all—the core work of the school—and make whatever alterations are possible to facilitate that core work and the professional growth it requires.

Another aspect of organizational life is that organizational procedures can become so routinized that they obscure the large purposes and values the school is pursuing. Teachers and students can forget the human significance of what their shared life together is all about. Human resource leaders have to continuously seek to refresh the vision of what the school is striving for and how that vision can energize the more mundane activities of the school day or week. That vision has to be rooted in a larger sense of human purpose and value that is intrinsic to the work they do together, that the journey of learning enables them to discover the marvelous intricacy of nature, the rich tapestry of culture, the complex challenges facing society, the human satisfactions of creativity, of friendships and of heroic strivings. That vision is what transforms the school from an organization into a human community.

Whether considered as organizations or communities, schools are also political environments. Politics implies power—who has more of it, what power is used for, how people organize to exert power, the concern for power to control versus collective power to do something worthwhile. Human resource leaders need to be concerned with empowerment, the facilitation of people to own themselves, to use their power with young people to draw them toward significant lives and significant learning. Again, the point is not to lose sight of the human dimension in all of this and to promote the positive side of political participation as an exercise in citizenship.

One cannot be a good citizen, however, and violate one's own and others' humanity. A human resource administrator must likewise embrace commitments to an ethical life. That means treating everyone in the school as a human being with care and compassion, treating them as citizens in their own right, with rights and responsibilities and engaging them in the ethical exercise of the common, core work of the school, namely authentic teaching and learning. Grounded in the general ethics of justice, care, and critique, human resource leaders need to attend to the specific ethical challenges that flow out of the work of educating the young. That work of educating is a human work as well as a work of public service for the good of the community. That requires educational leaders to orchestrate the resources, the structures, and the processes of the school within the ethical obligations of justice. That orchestration is usually carried on within the transactional ethics of negotiated agreements about what the nature of the work is and what is expected from the various members of the school community who all contribute to the carrying out of that work.

Educational leaders have to be humane, caring, and compassionate, even while appealing to the more altruistic motives of the teachers and students. Human resource leaders will insist that teachers connect the academic subjects of the curriculum to the human journey of their learners. The leader has to affirm the dignity and rights of students and teachers as autonomous citizens, even while appealing to their higher civic and democratic ideals. The leader has to acknowledge the demanding nature of teaching and learning, the steady work on assignments, the routinization of learning and teaching—even while appealing to the transformational possibilities of authentic learning in the individual and communal creation of their own humanity in the learning process. Finally, the educational leader has to acknowledge the ethics of organizational life, the fact that every organization imposes limitations on the freedom and creativity of all the individuals involved in the organization. Schools as organizations coordinate daily and weekly schedules that channel and focus everyone's effort on the core work of the school: the production of understanding of the world and of themselves and the exploration of the responsibilities membership in those worlds implies. That work imposes a daily discipline of cooperative action. Nevertheless, the human resource leader sees to it that the structures and procedures that support and channel the learning process reflect a concern for justice and fairness to all students, while also providing room for creativity and imagination needed for the work to succeed.

Human Resource Leadership as Distributed or Dense Leadership

The perspective of this book is that many people throughout the system share in the large task of human resource development. By including every teacher as a front-line human resource leader, we emphasize their role in the daily work with learners, and the need for them to connect the human agenda of the learners with the academic agenda of exploring and discovering the worlds of nature, culture, and society and the meanings those worlds contribute to their self-construction. The proactive cultivation and shaping of this kind of transformative learning defines the practice of teaching as a transformative agency that connects a deep moral, professional, and political significance to that work.

The collective leadership of teachers must struggle against the traditional culture of isolation in schools, a culture that encourages individual teachers to think of their classrooms as isolated silos where they are protected from the scrutiny of intrusive administrators and nosey colleagues. This is why the individual leadership of teachers needs the leadership of those others who work with groups within the teaching and support faculty as coaches, cluster leaders, department chairs, project directors, instructional supervisors, committee chairs, assistant principals, and principals. These are the human resource leaders of the collective effort of the teachers. These are the leaders who encourage collaboration around improving student learning, the team exploration of solutions and new perspectives, the sharing of effective teaching practices, the promotion of consistent depth in learning across and between grade levels. Their leadership is essential to provide the stimulation, support, encouragement, risk-taking, and organizational resources that build collective capacity and efficacy within the faculty at large.

Principals and assistant principals bring a school-wide perspective to the collaborative work of the various groups of teachers. Their leadership is needed to coordinate the work of the groups into a consistent horizontal and vertical pattern of performance that is responsive to the goals, core values, and the very mission of the school. They are the ones who must frequently articulate those goals, values, and mission in order to elevate the appreciation by the teachers and students of the significance their daily work. They are the ones who frequently arbitrate and negotiate conflicts within the community by referring to those goals, values and mission, and to the more particular policies that support them.

We can begin to appreciate, then, that human resource leadership at the school level should involve all the members of the professional staff in a consistent, and intentional focus on the core work of the school, namely the quality learning and human development of the young people entrusted to their care. At the local level, the principal should see him or herself as the leader of an organically integrated system of human resource development, a system that coordinates and supports all aspects of human resource development in the school. That leadership work can be seen as the essential leadership work of the principal.

At the district level, the superintendent can be viewed as the system-wide leader of human resource development, even though the administration of that system might be in the hands of a deputy or assistant superintendent. Under the leadership of the superintendent, teams of principals from the schools in the district can be brought together to explore the strengths and weaknesses of the district-wide system of human resource development in order to develop greater systemic coordination and support.

By bringing human resource leadership into its essential connection with the core work of the whole system, the superintendent will be signaling a focus on the human side of the whole schooling enterprise, and the integration of academic learning into this human dimension of the work of the schools. In providing this large and humanly appealing vision of the nature of their collective work together, this kind of systemic leadership can effect both the internal transformation of the work, and its translation into the social and human capital that the civic community seeks.

Conclusion

Those who have made the journey with this book will find the vision of human resource development as the essential focus of educational leadership throughout a given school system both appealing and possible of realization. At the outset, this journey was advertised as proposing an ideal. The argument has been, however, that unless we explore the ideal, we will tend to be satisfied with the all too prosaic practice of a series of administrative functions. That functional, technical character of the work cannot be dismissed. However, that technical aspect of the work, when incorporated into the larger view of the human resource development of the learners and the teachers, can be seen as saturated with value and significance derived from the vision and core mission of the school which it serves.

Obviously, the reality of schools presents a messy picture filled with unpredictability, human pain and misunderstanding, collisions of vested interests, as well as moments of growth, insight, and delight. The reality reveals many success stories, but still too many stories of distress and disappointment. The reality of schools is that they are ordinary sites of human striving, some of it self-seeking, some of it altruistic, some of it superficial, some of it potentially heroic. Inside the ordinariness of school life one can find extraordinary promise, often unfulfilled because never appreciated as possible, or unfulfilled because the routines of school life had smothered the expectation of extraordinary human achievements. The vision of the school should speak of the extraordinary possibilities for human achievement in our young people, as well as the extraordinary, though often unrealized talents of their teachers to nurture those possibilities. We should refuse to accept the current organization of schools into one-size-fits-all egg-crates as necessarily permanent. Those who embrace the ideals put forth in this book can reconstruct the way the schools organize and support learning so as to more fully realize those human ideals.

Likewise, the politics of school life do not have to reduce humans to the lowest common denominator of self-interest or to the power dynamics of controlling or being controlled. Human beings are a community of saints and sinners—though the sinners are usually the only ones making the headlines. There will be some who, for a variety of reasons, choose to be destructive forces in the community and who need to be referred to other social institutions. There will be many others who need more structured learning arrangements, at least until they can work more creatively and inventively on their learning tasks with others. Schools, however, do not need to be run like prisons or like military boot camps, nor, indeed, like business corporations. They can have much more in common with the dynamics to be found in healthy families, or with faith communities or other voluntary organizations in societies, where the politics involves much more mutuality and collaboration, where the good of each is tied up with the common good of all.

In short, the vision of educational leadership as human resource development can lead to as yet unrealized possibilities in many school systems, even though the vision will never be fully realized. Indeed, visions are never meant to be fully realized, for their nature is always to be out in front of us, calling our attention to yet unrealized possibilities. If we ever were to think a vision had been realized, we should take that as a warning signal that we were on the road to stagnation. Leadership from within this vision expects humans to make mistakes, to create messes. Nevertheless, it is out of the distress, frustration, and pain that we cause in a given circumstance that we can develop new perspectives that point us in a direction that we need to go. Isn't that what learning is all about, the gradual transformation of our own fragile and immature humanity into something more fully human? Lewis Mumford (1964) reminds us,

> Though we have succeeded brilliantly in the transformation of matter, far beyond the wildest dreams of the ancient alchemists, who would pretend that we have had any equivalent success in the transformation of (the human person)? (p. 498)

References

Preface

Callahan, R.E. (1962). *Education and the cult of efficiency.* Chicago: University of Chicago Press.

Duignan, P.A. (2010). Leading learning in Catholic school. Sydney, Australia: Duignan Educational & Professional Consulting Services.

Fuller, R.W. (2003). *Somebodies and nobodies: Overcoming the abuse of rank.* Gabriola Island, Canada: New Society Publishers.

Harris, A. (2008). *Distributed leadership: Developing tomorrow's leaders.* London: Routledge.

Leithwood, K. & Mascall, B. (2008). *Distributed leadership according to the evidence.* New York: Routledge.

Mayo, E. (1933). *The human problems of an industrial civilization.* New York: Macmillan.

Miles, M. (1965). Human relations or human resources? *Harvard Business Review, 43*(4), 148–163.

Spillane, J. (Ed.) (2007). *Distributed leadership in practice.* New York: Teachers College Press.

Taylor, F. (1911). *The principles of scientific management.* New York: Harper & Row.

Chapter 1

Dewey, J. (1916). *Democracy and education: An introduction to the philosophy of education.* New York: Macmillan.

Chapter 2

Arnett, J.J. (2004). *Emerging adulthood. The winding road from the late teens through the twenties.* New York: Oxford University Press.

Becker, E. (1971). *The birth and death of meaning* (second edition). New York: The Free Press.

Bonnet, M. & Cuypers, S. (2003). Autonomy and authenticity in education. In N. Blake, P. Smeyers, R. Smith, & P. Standish (Eds.), *The Blackwell guide to the philosophy of education* (pp. 326–340). Oxford, England: Blackwell.

Brophy, J. (Ed.) (2001). *Subject-specific instructional methods and activities.* Amsterdam: Elsevier Science.

Bruner, J. (1987). The transactional self. In J. Bruner & H. Haste (Eds.), *Making sense: The child's construction of the world* (pp. 81–96). New York: Methuen.

Bruner, J. (1990). *Acts of meaning.* Cambridge, MA: Harvard University Press.

Conn, W. E. (1977). Erik Erikson: The ethical orientation, conscience, and the Golden Rule. *Journal of Religious Education, 5*(2), 249–266.

Coté J. & Levine, C. (2002). *Identity formation, agency, and culture: A social psychological synthesis.* Mahwah, NJ: Erlbaum.

Egan, K. (1990). *Romantic understanding: The development of rationality and imagination, ages 8–15.* New York: Routledge.

Egan, K. (1997). *The educated mind: How cognitive tools shape our understanding.* Chicago: University of Chicago Press.

Egan, K. (1999). *Children's minds, talking rabbits & clockwork oranges: Essays on education.* New York: Teachers College Press.

Frawley, W. (1997). *Vygotsky and cognitive science: Language and the unification of the social and computational mind.* Cambridge, MA: Harvard University Press.

Freidman, L.J. (1999). *Identity's architect: A biography of Erik H. Erikson.* New York: Scribner.

Freire, P. (1998). *Teachers as cultural workers: Letters to those who dare to teach.* Trans. by D. Macedo, D. Koike, & A. Oliveira. Denver, CO: Westview Press.

Freud, A. (1968). Psychoanalysis and education, 1954. In *Indications for child analysis and other papers, 1945–1956. The writings of Anna Freud* (Vol 4, pp. 317–326). New York: International Universities Press.

Giddens, A. (1991). *Modernity and self-identity: Self and society in the late modern age.* Stanford, CA: Stanford University Press.

Goffman, E. (1959). *The presentation of self in everyday life.* Garden City, NY: Doubleday Anchor Books.

Hoare, C.H. (2002). *Erikson on development in adulthood: New insights from unpublished papers.* New York: Oxford University Press.

Hoover, K.R. (Ed) (2004). *The future of identity: Centennial reflections on the legacy of Erik Erikson.* Lanham, MD: Lexington Books.

Knowles, R.T. (1986). *Human development and human possibility: Erikson in the light Heidegger.* Lanham, MD: University Press of America.

McCarthy, E.D. (1996). *Knowledge as culture: The new sociology of knowledge.* London: Routledge.

Macdonald, J.B. (1971). A vision of a humane school. In J.G. Saylor & J.L. Smith (Eds.), *Barriers to humanness in the high school* (pp. 2–20). Washington, DC: Association of Supervision and Curriculum Development.

Nixon, J., Martin, J., McKeown, P., & Ransom, S. (1996). *Encouraging learning: Towards a theory of the learning school.* Buckingham, England: Open University Press.

Perkins, D. (1992). *Smart schools.* New York: The Free Press.

Pope, D.C. (2001). *"Doing school": How we are creating a generation of stressed out, materialistic, and miseducated students.* New Haven, CT: Yale University Press.

Reay, D. & William, D. (2001). "I'll be a nothing": Structure, agency, and the construction of identity through assessment. In J. Collins & D. Cook (Eds.), *Understanding learning: Influences and outcomes* (pp. 149–161). London: Paul Chapman Publishers and Open University Press.

Roazen, P. (1997). *Erik Erikson: The power and limits of a vision.* Northvale, NJ: Jason Aronson.

Sarason, S.B. (2004). *And what do you mean by learning?* Portsmouth, NH: Heinemann.

Shannon, P. (1995). *Text, lies, and videotape. Stories about life, literacy and learning.* Portsmouth, NH: Heinemann.

Shultz, J.S. & Cook-Sather, A. (2001). *In our own words: Students' perspectives on school.* Lanham, MD: Rowan & Littlefield.

Sprinthall, N.A. & Theis-Sprinthall, L. (1983). The teacher as adult learner: A cognitive-evelopmental view. In G. Griffin (Ed.), *Staff development*. Eighty Second Yearbook of the National Society for the Study of Education, Part II (pp. 13–35). Chicago: University of Chicago Press.

Starratt, R.J. (1990). *The drama of schooling/ the schooling of drama*. London: Falmer Press.

Stevens, R. (2008). *Erik H. Erikson: Explorer of identity and the life cycle*. New York: Palgrave Macmillan.

Taylor, C. (1991). *The ethics of authenticity*. Cambridge, MA: Harvard University Press.

Wallerstein, R.S. & Goldberger, L. (1998). *Ideas and identities: The life and work of Erik Erikson*. Madison, CT: International Universities Press.

Welchman, K. (2000). *Eik Erikson: His life, work and significance*. Philadelphia: Open University Press.

Wiles, M. (1983). *Children into pupils*. London: Routledge and Kegan Paul.

Chapter 3

Adams, P. (2004). Supporting teachers' professional development. In P.E. Holland (Ed.), *Beyond measure: Neglected elements of accountability* (pp. 101–132). Larchmont, NY: Eye on Education.

Augros, R.M. & Stanciu, G.N. (1987). *The new biology: Discovering the wisdom in nature*. Boston: New Science Library.

Bateson, G. (1979). *Mind and nature: A necessary unity*. New York: E.P. Dutton.

Berry, T.M. (1988). *The dream of the earth*. San Francisco: Sierra Club Books.

Bloom, H. (1998). *Shakespeare: The invention of the human*. London: Fourth Estate.

Delors, J., Al Mufti, I., Amagi, A., Carneiro, R., Chung, F. Geremek, B., et al. (1996). *Learning: The treasure within—Report to UNESCO of the International Commission on Education for the Twenty-first Century*. Paris: United Nations Educational, Scientific, and Cultural Organization.

Danielson, C. & McGreal, T.L (2000). *Teacher evaluation to enhance professional practice*. Alexandria, VA: Association for Supervision and Curriculum Development.

Eiseley, L. (1957). *The immense journey*. New York: Vantage Books.

Eiseley, L. (1962). *The mind as nature*. New York: Charles Scribner's Sons.

Elmore, R.F. (2000). *Building a new structure for school leadership*. Washington, DC: The Albert Shanker Institute.

Elmore, R.F. (2004). Agency, reciprocity, and accountability in democratic education. Cambridge, MA: Harvard University and Consortium for Policy and Research in Education.

Elmore R.F. (n.d.). Improving the instructional core. Harvard University. Retrieved from http://www.iowa.gov/educate/ecpd//index.php?option=com_docman&task=doc_details&gid=15&Itemid=99999999

Guskey, T.R. & Huberman, M. (Eds.). (1995). *Professional development in education: New paradigms and practices*. New York: Teachers College Press.

Hargreaves, A. & Fink, D. (2006). *Sustainable leadership*. San Francisco: Jossey-Bass.

Joyce, B.R. & Showers, B. (2002). *Student achievement through staff development* (third edition). Alexandria, VA: Association for Supervision and Curriculum Development.

Macintyre, A. (1981). *After virtue*. Notre Dame, IN: University of Notre Dame Press.

Morin, E. (1999). *Seven complex lessons in education for the future*. Trans. by N. Poller. Paris: United Nations Educational, Scientific, and Cultural Organization.

Polanyi, M. (1966). *The tacit dimension*. Garden City, NY: Doubleday.

Prigogine, I. & Stengers, I. (1984). *Order out of chaos; Man's new dialogue with nature*. New York: Bantam Books.

Schon, D.A. (1987). *Educating the reflective practitioner: Toward a new design for teaching and learning in the professions*. San Francisco: Jossey-Bass.

Seilstad, G.A. (1989). *At the heart of the web: The inevitable genesis of intelligent life*. New York: Harcourt Brace.

Sergiovanni, T.J. (2001). *The principalship: A reflective practice perspective*. Boston: Allyn & Bacon.

Wiske, M.S. (Ed.). (1998). *Teaching for understanding: Linking research with practice*. San Francisco: Jossey Bass.

Zohar, D. & Marshall, I. (1994). *The quantum society*. London: Harper.

Chapter 4

Eisenstadt, S.N. (Ed.). (1968). *Max Weber on charisma and institution building: Selected papers*. Chicago: University of Chicago Press.

Giddens, A. (1986). *The constitution of society: Outline of the theory of structuration*. Berkeley, CA: University of California Press.

Hoy, W.K. & Sweetland, S.R. (2001). Designing better schools: The meaning and nature of enabling school structure. *Educational Administration Quarterly, 37*, 296–321.

Perkins D. (1992). *Smart schools. Better thinking and learning for every child*. New York: The Free Press.

Pope, D.C. (2001). *"Doing School": How we are creating a generation of stressed out, materialistic, and miseducated students*. New Haven, CT: Yale University Press.

Powell, A.G., Farrar, E., & Cohen, D.K. (1985). *The shopping mall high school: Winners and losers in the educational marketplace*. Boston: Houghton Mifflin.

Rousseau J.J. (1979). *Emile: On education* (Trans. by Allan Bloom) New York: Basic Books.

Senge, P.M. (1990). *The fifth discipline: The art and practice of the learning organization*. New York: Doubleday.

Starratt, R.J. (1995). *Leaders with vision: The quest for school renewal*. Thousand Oaks, CA: Corwin Press.

Chapter 5

Bandura, A. (1997). *Self-efficacy: The exercise of control*. New York: Freeman.

Barber, B. (1998). *A passion for democracy: American essay*. Princeton, NJ: Princeton University Press.

Barton, K.C. & Levstik, L.S. (2004). *Teaching history for the common good*. Mahwah, NJ: Erlbaum.

Beck, U., Giddens, A., & Lash, S. (1994). *Reflexive modernization: Politics, tradition and aesthetics in the modern social order*. Stanford, CA: Stanford University Press.

Becker, E. (1967). *Beyond alienation: A philosophy of education for the crisis of democracy*. New York; G. Braziller.

Blasé, J. & Blasé, J. (2001). *Empowering teachers: What successful principals do*. Thousand Oaks, CA: Corwin Press.

Block, J.E. (2002). *A nation of agents: The American path to a modern self and society*. Cambridge, MA: Belknap Press of Harvard University Press.

Broudy, H.S., Smith, B.O., & Burnett, J.R. (1964). *Democracy and excellence in American secondary education: A study in curriculum theory*. Chicago: Rand McNally.

Bryk, A.S. & Schneider, B. (2002). *Trust in schools: A core resource for improvement*. New York: Russell Sage Foundation.

Burns, J.M. (1978). *Leadership*. New York: Harper Colophon Books.

Comer, J.P., Haynes, N.M., Joyner, E.T., & Ben-Avie, M. (Eds.). (1996). *Rallying the whole village: The Comer process for reforming education*. New York: Teachers College Press.

Dewey, J. (1916). *Democracy and education*. New York: Macmillan.

Eisenstadt, S.N. (1968). Introduction: Charisma and institution building: Max Weber and Modern Sociology. In S.N. Eisenstadt (Ed.), *Max Weber: Charisma and institution building* (pp. ix–lvi). Chicago and London: University of Chicago Press.

Furman G.C. & Starratt, R.J. (2002). Leadership for democratic community in schools. In J. Murphy (Ed.), *The educational leadership challenge: Redefining leadership for the 21st century* (pp. 105–133). Chicago: National Society for the Study of Education, University of Chicago Press.

Horn, R. A. (2008). The essential question concerning the promotion of democracy through education. Paper presented at the Annual Meeting of the American Educational Research Association, March, New York City.

Hoy, W.K. (2002). Faculty trust: A key to student achievement. *Journal of School Public Relations, 23*(2), 88–103.

Jenlink, P.M. (Ed.). (2008). *Dewey's Democracy and Education revisited: Contemporary discourses for democratic education and leadership.* Lanham, MD: Rowman & Littlefield.

King, M.L. Jr. (1967). *Where do we go from here: Chaos or community?* New York: Harper & Row.

Oakes J. & Quartz, K. H. (Eds.) (1995). *Creating new educational communities.* Chicago: NSSE & University of Chicago Press.

Oakes, J., Quartz, K.H., Ryan, S., & Lipton, M. (2000). *Becoming good American schools: The struggle for civic virtue in educational reform.* San Francisco: Jossey-Bass.

Starratt, R.J. (2001). Democratic leadership theory in late modernity: An oxymoron or ironic possibility? *International Journal of Leadership in Education, 4*(4), 333–352.

Starratt, R.J. (2008). Democracy and Education revisited: A continuing leadership agenda. In P. M. Jenlink (Ed.), *Dewey's Democracy and Education revisited: Contemporary discourses for democratic education and leadership* (pp. 52–70). Lanham, MD: Rowman & Littlefield.

Swanson, M.C., Meehan, H., & Hubbard, L. (1995). The AVID classroom; academic and social support for low-achieving students. In J. Oakes, & K.H. Quartz (Eds.), *Creating new educational communities; Ninety-fourth yearbook of the National Society for the Study of Education* (pp. 53–69). Chicago: The University of Chicago Press.

Chapter 6

Adams, J.E. & Kirst, M.W. (1999). New demands and concepts for educational accountability: Striving for results in an era of excellence. In J. Murphy & K. Seashore Louis (Eds.), *Handbook of research on educational administration* (pp. 463–489). San Francisco: Jossey-Bass.

Ashton, P.T. & Webb, R.B. (1986). *Making a Difference: Teachers' sense of efficacy and student achievement.* New York: Longman.

Coleman, J.S. (1966). *Equality of Educational Opportunity.* Washington, DC: Office of Education, National Center for Educational Statistics.

Danielson, C. & McGreal, T.L. (2000). *Teacher evaluation: To enhance professional practice.* Alexandria, VA: Association for Supervision and Curriculum Development.

Elmore, R. F. (2008). Improving the instructional core. Retrieved from http://www.iowa.gov/educate/ecpd//index.php?option=com_docman&task=doc_details&gid=15&Itemid=99999999

Furman, G. (2003). What is leadership for? *UCEA Review, 55*(1), 1–6.

Haynes, F. (1998). *The ethical school.* London: Routledge.

Hehir, T. (2002). Eliminating abelism in education. *Harvard Educational Review, 72* (1), 1–32.

Hursthouse, R. (1999). *On virtue ethics.* Oxford, England: Oxford University Press.

Maxcy, S.J. (2002). *Ethics of school leadership.* Lanham, MD: Scarecrow Press.

Nash, R.J. (2002). *"Real World" ethics; Frameworks for educators and human service professionals.* (second edition). New York: Teachers College Press.

Oakes, J. (1985). *Keeping track: How schools structure inequality.* New Haven, CT: Yale University Press.

Polanyi, M. (1966). *The tacit dimension.* Garden City, NY: Doubleday.

Sergiovanni, T.J. & Starratt, R.J. (2006). *Supervision: A redefinition* (eighth edition). New York: McGraw-Hill.

Shapiro, J.P. & Stefkovich, J.A. (2001). *Ethical leadership and decision making in education.* Mahwah, NJ: Erlbaum.

Starratt, R.J. (1991). Building an ethical school: A theory for practice in educational leadership. *Educational Administration Quarterly 27*(2), 195–202.

Starratt, R.J. (1998). Grounding moral educational leadership in the morality of teaching and learning. *Leading and Managing, 4*(4), 243–255.

Starratt, R.J. (2003). Opportunity to learn and the accountability agenda. *Phi Delta Kappan, 58*(4), 298–303.

Starratt, R.J. (2004). *Ethical leadership.* San Francisco: Jossey-Bass.

Starratt, R.J. (2007). Leading a community of learners: Learning to be moral by engaging the morality of learning. *Educational Management, Administration, and Leadership 35*(2), 165–183.

Strike, K.A., Haller, E.J., & Soltis, J.F. (1998). *The ethics of school administration.* New York: Teachers College Press.

Walker, R.L. & Ivanhoe, P.J. (Eds.). (2007). *Working virtue: Virtue ethics and contemporary moral problems.* New York: Oxford University Press.

Chapter 7

Council of Chief State School Officers. (1996). *Interstate School Leaders Licensure Consortium: Standards for School Leaders.* Retrieved from http:/www.ccsso.org/publications/details.cfm?PublicationID=87

Council of Chief State School Officers. (2008). *Educational Leadership Policy Standards: 2008. As adapted by the National Policy Board for Educational Administration.* Retrieved from http:/www.ccsso.org/publications/details.cfm?PublicationID=365

Danielson, C. & McGreal, T.L. (2000). *Teacher evaluation to enhance professional practice.* Alexandria, VA: Association for Supervision and Curriculum Development.

Scriven, M. (1990). Can research-based teacher evaluations be saved? *Journal of Personnel Evaluation in Education 4*, 19–32.

Stodolsky, S. (1984). Teacher evaluation: The limits of looking. *Educational Researcher 13*(9), 11–19.

Chapter 8

Mumford, L. (1964). The forces of life. In P. Goodman (Ed.), *Seeds of liberation* (pp. 498–507). New York: George Braziller.

Index

A

Academic self-image, 18
Accountability, responsibility, 100–101
Action, 15–16
  ego, 25–28, *26*
Administrators, self-esteem, 5
Adolescents, *17*, 18
Affective clarity, 3–4
Agency, 15–16
  ego, relationship, 27
  organizational setting, 58–60
Assistant principals, human resource
    leadership, 132
Assumptions, 63–65, 66
Authenticity
  change, 92
  characterized, 30, 31
  Charles Taylor's ethic, 31
  culture, 31
  learning, 30–32
  values, 31
  virtue, 91–93
  vs. mindless inauthenticity, 31
Authentic learning, 101
  district superintendents, 106–107
Autonomy, *17, 17, 22, 23*

B

Beliefs, 63–65, 66

C

Capacity-building, 97
Change, authenticity, 92

Coalition building
  from coalitions to community, 85–87
  politics, 82–84
Cognitive clarity, 3–4
Community, 85–87
Concrete-operational thinking, 28–29
Conflict, politics
  expression, 82
  negotiation of, 82
Conflict resolution, 124–125
Content knowledge, 39–41
  transformative power, 41–42
Continuous learning, 43
Contract negotiations, 125–126
Creativity
  organizational setting, 54–58
  Weber, Max, 54–58
Crisis, 16
Critical presence, 99–100
Cultivation of learning, 37–39
  as metaphor, 37
Culture, 6, 61–62
  authenticity, 31
  district superintendents, change within
    the district office, 106–107
  schools
    human capital, 128–129
    social capital, 128–129
Curriculum
  basic justification, 3–4
  of community, 3–4
  learners, *49*, 49–50
  learning, 43

Curriculum (*continued*)
   teachers, 47–48, *48*
Curriculum knowledge
   abstracted from learner's cultural and
      psychodynamic biography, 28
   reflective learnings, 28

D
Democracy, 75
   defined, 77
   democratic ideal, 76–78
      conflicts over interpretations, 78–79
   human resource development, 77–78
   response of realpolitik, 84–85
   U.S. since September 11, 2001, 76–77
   versions, 76
Dense leadership, human resource
   leadership, 131–133
Disempowerment, 74–75
Distributed leadership, human resource
   leadership, 131–133
District director, Human Resource
   Administration, 107–108
District superintendents
   authentic learning, 106–107
   culture, change within the district
      office, 106–107
   district team, 106–107
   human resource development, as
      leader of leaders, 105–107
   human resource leadership, 132
   principals, 106–107
   role, 106
District support systems, human resource
   development, 110–126
Drama, as metaphor, 2–9
Due process
   learners, 119
   teachers, 119

E
Education, *See also* Specific type
   basic relationships, 5
   humanity of, 8
   metaphor for life, 5
   realistic mental model, 8–9
   uses, 3
   virtue, 89–91
Efficacy, 98
Ego, 15–16, 27
   action, 25–28, *26*
   agency, relationship, 27
   I, relationship, 25–28, *26*

meaning making, 25–28, *26*
   understanding, relationship, 27
Ego identity, 30–32
Empowerment, 74–75
Enabling presence, 96–98
Erikson, Erik
   human development, 15–33
   academic self-image, 18
   adolescents, *17*, 18
   autonomy, 17, *17*, *22*, *23*
   cautions against simplifications,
      22–24
   connecting learning to authenticity,
      30–32
   ego, 27
   generativity, *17*, 21, *22*, *23*
   gradual integration of earlier stage
      strengths, *23*
   identity, *17*, 18, *22*, *23*
   industry, *23*
   initiative, *23*
   integration, *23*
   integrity, *17*, 21, *22*
   intimacy, 20–21, *22*, *23*
   learning occasioned by crisis, 16
   linking school learnings to life-cycle
      challenges, 24–30
   marriage, 20–21
   psychological health *vs.* illness, 15
   relationships, 17
   roles, 24–25
   self-identity, 19, *22*
   self-transcendence, 19, 20
   sexual identity, 18
   stages, 16–17, *17*
   teachers' pedagogical approach to
      curriculum, 32
   trust, 17, *17*, *22*, 22–23, *23*
   wisdom, *17*, 21, *22*
   scholarly credentials, 15
Ethics, 89–91, 130–131
   general ethics *vs.* applied, professional
      ethics, 90
Expression, 15–16

F
Formal operations, 29
   desirability of, 29–30
Freedom
   organizational setting, 54–58
   teachers, 54–58
   Weber, Max, 54–58
Freud, Sigmund, human development, 15

G
Generativity, *17,* 21, *22, 23*
Goals, 63

H
Hiring, 114–117
Hospitals, 58–59
Human beings, 1–2
  journey of, 3–4
Human capital, 127
Human development
  Erikson, Erik, 15–33
  academic self-image, 18
  adolescents, *17,* 18
  autonomy, 17, *17, 22, 23*
  cautions against simplifications,
    22–24
  connecting learning to authenticity,
    30–32
  ego, 27
  generativity, *17,* 21, *22, 23*
  gradual integration of earlier stage
    strengths, *23*
  identity, *17,* 18, *22, 23*
  industry, *23*
  initiative, *23*
  integration, *23*
  integrity, *17,* 21, *22*
  intimacy, 20–21, *22, 23*
  learning occasioned by crisis, 16
  linking school learnings to life-cycle
    challenges, 24–30
  marriage, 20–21
  psychological health *vs.* illness, 15
  relationships, 17
  roles, 24–25
  self-identity, 19, *22*
  self-transcendence, 19, 20
  sexual identity, 18
  stages, 16–17, *17*
  teachers' pedagogical approach to
    curriculum, 32
  trust, 17, *17, 22,* 22–23, *23*
  wisdom, *17,* 21, *22*
  Freud, Sigmund, 15
  geography, working within, 13–33
  need for understanding, 14–15
  organic interpenetration, 127–134
  professional development,
    foregrounding human
    development, 35–52
  teachers' pedagogical approach to
    curriculum, 32

  theory, 15–33
Human Resource Administration, district
  director, 107–108
Human resource development
  democracy, 77–78
  district superintendent, 105–107
  district support systems, 110–126
  district system, 105–126
  goals, 13–14
  leaders of leaders, 105–126
  moral dimension, 89–104
  organizational structures and
    processes, 102–103
  organizational setting
    leadership work–management work
      integration, 67–70, *68*
    managing specifics, 69–70
    vision, 67–69
  politics, 73–88
    from coalitions to community,
      85–87
    democratic politics, 81–88
  principals, 108–109
  terrain mapping, 14
  virtues, 89–104
Human resource leadership
  assistant principals, 132
  characterized, 2, 13–14
  dense leadership, 131–133
  distributed leadership, 131–133
  educating community of adults,
    8–9
  interdependence of six dimensions,
    129–131
  most basic dimension of work, 8
  organizational setting, 53–71
    organizational leadership vision,
      61–66
    organization life blood analogy,
      53–54
    personal fulfillment *vs.*
      organizational demands, 54–58
    tension between structure and
      agency in organizations, 58–60
  parents, 80
  principals, 132
  superintendents, 132
  teachers, 132
  virtue, 89–91

I
I, ego, relationship, 25–28, *26*
Id, 15–16

Identity, *17*, 18, *22, 23*
  performative school, 9
  students, 9
Induction of teachers, 117–118
Industry, *23*
Influence, politics, 82–84
Initiative, *23*
Integration, *23*
Integrity, knowledge, 101–102
Intimacy, 20–21, *22, 23*

K
King, Martin Luther Jr., 88
Knowledge, *See also* Specific type
  as dependent, 39–44
  as independent, 39–44
  integrity, 101–102
  as interior, 39–44
  learner, taking knowledge, 41
  learning, relationship, 38
  teacher, taking knowledge, 41

L
Leadership
  study of, 13
  virtues, 90–104
Learners
  active *vs.* passive, 38–39
  curriculum, *49*, 49–50
  due process, 119
  organizational setting, 55–56, 57
  taking knowledge, 41
Learning
  authenticity, 30–32, 101
  cultivation of, 37–39
  curriculum, 43
  knowledge, relationship, 38
  meaning making, 27
  noun *vs.* verb, 38
  psycho-social model, 25–28, *26*
Listening presence, 96
Love, power, relationship, 88

M
Marriage, 20–21
Meaning making, 15–16
  ego, 25–28, *26*
  learning, 27
Meanings, 64, 66
Mentoring, teachers, 118–119
Moral dimension, human resource
    development, 89–104
  organizational structures and

  processes, 102–103
Myths, 64, 66

N
Nature, 6

O
Onion Model of Schools, 61–66, *62, 65,*
  66
Organizational setting
  creativity, 54–58
  freedom, 54–58
  human resource development
    leadership work–management work
      integration, 67–70, *68*
    managing specifics, 69–70
    vision, 67–69
  human resource leadership, 53–71
    organizational leadership vision,
      61–66
    organization life blood analogy,
      53–54
    personal fulfillment *vs.*
      organizational demands, 54–58
    tension between structure and
      agency in organizations, 58–60
  learners, 55–56, 57
  paradox of organizational life, 57–58
  schools, 59–60

P
Parents, human resource leadership, 80
Performative school, 9–12
  identity, 9
  important learnings, 10
  promoting *vs.* threatening life, 10–11
  relationality, 9–10
  variety of performances, 11
Piaget, Jean, 28–29
Policy, 63
Politics
  characterized, 81
  coalition building, 82–84
  conflict
    expression, 82
    negotiation of, 82
  human resource development, 73–88
    from coalitions to community,
      85–87
  democratic politics, 81–88
  influence, 82–84
  negative connotations, 81
  positive view, 81

power, 82–84
  response of realpolitik, 84–85
  sociality, 73–76
Power, 74–75, 130
  love, relationship, 88
  politics, 82–84
Presence
  characterized, 93
  virtue, 93–100
    affirming presence, 99–100
    critical presence, 99–100
    enabling presence, 96–98
    listening presence, 96
Principals, 108–109
  district superintendents, 106–107
  human resource development, 108–109
  human resource leadership, 132
  role, 108–109
  teachers, 109
  vision statement, 109
Probationary status, teachers, 122–123
Professional competence
  clarifying focus on, 36–37
  teachers, 36–37
Professional development, 123, 129
  foregrounding human development, 35–52
  teachers, cultivation of human development, 35–52
  teaching model, implications for teachers' growth, 51–52
Professional ethics, 90

R
Realpolitik, 84–85
Recruitment, 112–114
  planning, 110–111
Reflective learnings, curriculum knowledge, 28
Relationality, 73–74
  performative school, 9–10
Responsibility
  accountability, 100–101
  virtue, 100–103
Roles, characterized, 24–25

S
Schools, *See also* Specific type
  basic relationships, 5
  characteristics, 59–60
  culture
    human capital, 128–129

social capital, 128–129
  drama metaphor, 2–9
  humanity of, 8
  internal human and social capital, 128–134
  internal politics, 81
  metaphor for life, 5
  Onion Model of Schools, 61–66, *62, 65, 66*
  organizational setting, 59–60
  realistic mental model, 8–9
  run like business corporations, 78–79
  as the state in action, 79–80
  uses, 3
  vision, 61
Self-esteem
  administrators, 5
  teachers, 5
Self-identity, 19, *22*
Self-transcendence, 19, 20
Sexual identity, 18
Social capital, 127–128
  internal, 128
Social contract, 75
Sociality, politics, 73–76
Society, 6–7
Spirit of efficacy, 98
Standardized academic tests, 78–79
Structure, organizational setting, 58–60
Structure-agency dialectic, 58–60
Students
  identity, 9
  place in world, 3–4
Superego, 15–16
Superintendents, *See* District superintendents

T
Teacher evaluation, 102–103, 119–123
Teacher-leadership committees, 96–97
Teachers
  characterized, 35–36
  curriculum, 47–48, *48*
  due process, 119
  educating community of adults, 8–9
  freedom, 54–58
  growth, 7–8
  human development, teachers' pedagogical approach to curriculum, 32
  human resource leadership, 132
  as human resources, 7–8
  mentoring, 118–119

Teachers (*continued*)
  new, 117–118
  principals, 109
  probationary status, 122–123
  professional competence, 36–37
  professional development, cultivation
    of human development, 35–52
  self-esteem, 5
  as the state educating its citizens,
    79–80
  taking knowledge, 41
  termination, 122–123
Teaching model, *44,* 44–51, *45, 48, 49*
  dialogue between students and subject
    matter, *49,* 49–50
  professional development, implications
    for teachers' growth, 51–52
  relationships within teaching-learning
    process, *44,* 44–45
  teacher's dialogical relationship with
    learners, *45,* 45–47
  teacher's knowledge of curriculum,
    47–48, *48*
Termination, teachers, 122–123
Test scores, 78–79, 100–101
Transformation, 134
Trust, 17, *17, 22,* 22–23, *23*
Tutoring, 56

U
Understanding, ego, relationship, 27

V
Values, authenticity, 31
Virtue
  authenticity, 91–93
  education, 89–91
  human resource development, 89–104
  human resource leadership, 89–91
  presence, 93–100
    affirming presence, 99–100
    critical presence, 99–100
    enabling presence, 96–98
    listening presence, 96
  responsibility, 100–103
Virtue ethics, 89–91
Vision, 67–69, 130
  articulation, 64
  communal, 64
  human resource leadership, 61–66
  Onion Model of Schools, 61–66, *62,*
    65, 66
  schools, 61
Vision statement, 65
  principals, 109
Voluntary associations, 55

W
Weber, Max
  creativity, 54–58
  freedom, 54–58
Wisdom, *17,* 21, *22*

eBooks – at www.eBookstore.tandf.co.uk

A library at your fingertips!

eBooks are electronic versions of printed books. You can store them on your PC/laptop or browse them online.

They have advantages for anyone needing rapid access to a wide variety of published, copyright information.

eBooks can help your research by enabling you to bookmark chapters, annotate text and use instant searches to find specific words or phrases. Several eBook files would fit on even a small laptop or PDA.

NEW: Save money by eSubscribing: cheap, online access to any eBook for as long as you need it.

Annual subscription packages

We now offer special low-cost bulk subscriptions to packages of eBooks in certain subject areas. These are available to libraries or to individuals.

For more information please contact webmaster.ebooks@tandf.co.uk

We're continually developing the eBook concept, so keep up to date by visiting the website.

www.eBookstore.tandf.co.uk